The Splintered Cross

Mending the Broken Parish

Bringing Cutting-Edge Methods to Wounded Christian Communities

By

Anne Katherine

www.1annekatherine.com

ISBN: 0692367047

ISBN-13: 978-0692367049 (Soulpath Press)

Books by Anne Katherine

Boundaries: Where You End and I Begin
Anatomy of a Food Addiction
Where to Draw the Line
When Misery Is Company
Your Appetite Switch
Lick It!
How to Make Almost Any Diet Work
Boundaries in an Overconnected World

DEDICATION

To Christian communities I have loved:
The Cursillo Community, Atlanta, Georgia, & North Carolina
Education for Ministry, (University of the South), Atlanta, Georgia
St. Cyprian's Episcopal Church, Franklin, North Carolina
Wallingford Methodist Church, Seattle, Washington
St. Stephen's Episcopal Church, Oak Harbor, Washington
St. Augustine's in-the-Woods Episcopal Church, Freeland, Washington

And to the Churches that taught me to love Christian community:
St. Luke's Episcopal Church, Atlanta, Georgia
Bethel United Church of Christ, Evansville, Indiana

Table of Contents

ACKNOWLEDGMENTS

Yvonne Agazarian is that rare combination of scholar, thinker, researcher, and empathic practitioner whose brilliance has brought us a new paradigm for transforming human potential into actualization. Her body of work is enormous, and I hope her reach will become infinite.

I am grateful to Dr. Agazarian, and also to Dr. Susan Gantt and Dr. Claudia Byram, for the privilege of being one of their students and for all the ways they, together, have enriched my life and work.

The organization that researches and teaches this powerful and comprehensive work is the Systems-Centered® Training and Research Institute, Inc. This book adapts their methods for use with a Christian community.

Many Thanks

I am fortunate that a group of friends, long-standing and on the new side, have become a sort of fan club, cheering my accomplishments, offering honest responses to this cover or that cover, and reading various incarnations of the material. I honestly feel their well-intentioned support and know, as I face the desktop, that I am truly not alone. Thank you, Friends and Fans. You make a difference.

Heartfelt thanks also to Dr. Thomas Johnson, professor of religious studies (ret.), George Fox University, and man of deep integrity, for being my first reader, offering excellent suggestions, and protecting me from heresy.

1 SCHISMS

Josie and Kara were best Christian friends. They'd cooked casseroles, polished pews, and wiped baby bottoms together for umpteen years. Then, suddenly, they didn't even wave at each other from opposite sides of the parking lot. (It's a really small parking lot.)

I felt the impact of the split as I walked to the little chapel that was our temporary (for years) church home during the rupture. I noticed that I was hesitating before acknowledging other people heading uphill toward the two sanctuaries.

Were they our congregation or those other people?

How ridiculous, I chastised myself. We are all Christian. We're all the same Protestant faith. I started waving, even to people on the other side of the divide. Some at least smiled. Some looked away.

Tragic.

If we had cards, I'd be a card-carrying Christian. Beyond my deep relationship with the Heavenly Host, I believe in the ideal of the Christian community. Throughout my life, I've belonged to a variety of churches and have loved several church communities.

But we have a weakness and I've seen it splinter and even rip apart tightly bonded communities, upsetting lovely people and turning well-meaning members into factions.

Throughout our land, mini-civil wars are being fought on hallowed ground. Clergy might be the generals or the targets.

Brother might be aligned against sister, child against parent, wife on one side, spouse on the other, as these skirmishes rattle parish halls.

What's it all about? Are we fighting ecclesial battles as important as the Great Apostasy, as shattering as the Council of Ephesus, as revolutionary as Golgotha? I don't think so. We might be standing on theoretical principles, but I think underneath that floor is a basement.

Answers?

I've observed various remedies applied to these schisms, even those going so far as to involve legal action. And my heart wept, because as a retired therapist with 40 years of experience, I knew there was another path, one that could lead to a breakthrough for all involved.

So, I ask you to slow down, give the unfolding of these words a chance, and watch as I build a bridge to another possibility.

2   DDT

Disappointment

People have a variety of reasons for joining a Christian community. We might suppose that the primary one is to facilitate one's connection to God, but some members might be there also or only for fellowship, for education, because it is what is done in that culture, because a parent or spouse wants them there, to find a decent mate, or even to advance themselves politically or professionally.

Sooner or later, a Christian community will be disappointing. We expect a lot of religious communities and their leaders, more than we expect of other gatherings of humans. We hold them, consciously or unconsciously, to a higher ideal.

My first cousin, thrice removed, was a nun. On a rare furlough, she came to Thanksgiving with Sister M. I thought they would be generous, kind, and sunny, so was surprised that Sister M beat me out for the last cookie and narrowed her eyes like *I* was the greedy guts. I was shocked. I didn't expect a nun to have a secular habit. Just seven years old and I already expected a professional Christian to be a better person.

When we get disappointed, then what? How will we handle it?

Difference

First Park Church makes a point of inclusiveness. Second Boulevard Church is proud of taking a stand against those "other" people. One man's sin is another man's sufferance.

We've survived thanks to our lightning-fast identification of differences. A bent branch outside the family cave, the subtle scent of a long-toothed tiger, the wind moaning a different tune at the forward edge of a storm—on the alert we went, reacting rapidly, to preserve ourselves and our people.

So, we are programmed. We react to a difference, sometimes before we've even identified what the difference is.

In the American culture, a sizable population has deliberately educated itself to calm that brain patterning—opening doors instead of barring them. We see, in our young, an acceptance of differences that we senior folk had to work to achieve. This is a cultural advance.

However, our programming still stands, and as we encounter differences, we register them and classify them on a scale from just noticeably different to too much difference.

Just Noticeable Difference   Too Great a Difference

My fashionable friend's facility with scarves wows me. I didn't get the fashionista gene, so her ability to fling a scarf around her shoulders and look like a million bucks is a noticeable difference. It's interesting, exciting even. Although why it looks like a remnant when I do it mystifies me.

On the other hand, when someone tailgates me on our whale-stomach-dark curvy country road as I'm twelfth in a line of cars (like, where does he think I can go), I get irritated. Doesn't the idiot know this is deer country? You can tell, by my characterization of this other rude and thoughtless human being, that this is too great a difference.

Differences show up in obvious ways of course—race, gender, age, ethnicity. And the Christian communities I've known have made an admirable effort to open arms and to promote equity. But differences also show up in opinions, responses, edicts, types of sermons, varying degrees of people skills, variety of life experience, and interpretation of religious matters.

Here we can get into trouble. A just noticeable difference in Biblical interpretation can lead to a spicy discussion. Too great a difference, one that lays a Mason-Dixon line that puts some in and others out, can lead to opposing camps.

So a challenge in the Christian community is how to handle too great a difference.

Triggers

Joy was washing the dishes and Sal was feeding the cat.

"Ouch!" Joy cried, and then pulled her hand out of the dishwater. Blood trickled redly down her finger. With hot energy, Joy said, "I hate that you put knives into the sink and then hide them with dishes."

"I don't deliberately hide the knives," Sal said angrily.

Joy shouted, "You don't even care that I'm hurt!"

"You think I don't care?"

"I've asked you," she said, "like 700 times, to not put knives in the dishpan. And you did it again."

Joy grabbed a bit of paper towel and pressed it to the cut, then added, "Do you want me to go bleeding to the hospital, holding my finger in a baggie?"

"You don't have to say it like that. Now I have that image in my head. Why would you put such a horrible image in my head?"

The cat ran out of the kitchen.

An excerpt from a pending book by Anne Katherine, *Letters to a New Couple.*

What happened?

Joy and Sal both were triggered into an exaggerated response.

Anyone who is or has been married has been triggered. A trigger is a hot button, and we all have them. Some of us have lots of them.

A trigger leads to a set of patterned behaviors, like those arguments we have over and over again with relatively few changes in dialogue. We could simply record the argument and play it the next time, inserting key words like, socks on the floor, losing the keys *again*, always late, or you don't care about my birthday. You probably wish I hadn't even been born. I do!

(Oops. That example got away from me.)

Most of the time, a trigger is innocently or thoughtlessly tripped, although a few years of marriage gives us the ability to deliberately detonate the other person's temper.

Marriage isn't, of course, the only venue where we get triggered. Any relationship with longevity will run into a situation where one or both people are triggered. And if one or both people don't recognize the canned environment and/or don't know what to do with it, it can fracture the relationship, perhaps permanently.

So what happens in a church if the pastor is triggered—or a leader or group of church leaders, or a subset of the community is triggered—into an enhanced reaction? It depends on their level of self awareness, skill, ability to let themselves be helped by someone who does recognize the subtext, and something else. (Next chapter coming soon.)

Not surprisingly, triggers backfire. One person gets triggered and his snap response sets off a trigger in the other person. These volleys can escalate the situation fast.

It takes discipline to slow everything down and skill to dismantle the mine field that has been planted.

And here's something to think about: the content of triggered dialogue and actions is real and it isn't real. But it looks totally real.

A part of most triggered behavior has to do with our own, sometimes deeply planted, issues. It looks very real to us, but that is due to the fact that we are now seeing the situation through a filter. This filter consists of long-standing issues that are very familiar in our own lives. The filter makes it look real, but the part that is filtered may not be real. And we may not be able to see the filter, so we may not know that our vision is awry.

Sussing out what is real and what isn't—that's where skill is needed.

DDT

Disappointment, differences, and triggers, the DDT that can poison a parish.

Something can be done. We'll get there.

3   THE AUTHORITY PHASE

Human relationships go through phases. Unless they get stuck. The three phases of human system development are:[1]

- Authority
- Intimacy
- Interdependent Love, Work, and Play (Productivity)[2]

The authority phase is a big one and has numerous subphases, each of which shows up in a predictable order that must be handled if relationships are to advance. The achievement of true intimacy is possible only when the authority phase is successfully traversed.

If you think about it, this makes sense. Only when we are comfortable with authority, when we know how to appropriately take and give authority, can we let ourselves risk intimacy.

The authority phase is not just about who's in charge. It's about far more complex processes:

- How we make room for ourselves, regardless of what other people are doing
- Catching ourselves in the act of putting ourselves under the command of someone else based on our own thoughts
- Noticing when we're traveling to the future, and letting an

---

[1] (Agazarian and Gantt, Autobiography 2000), pp. 208-209.

[2] Numerous social scientists have identified three to five stages of group development. Alfred North Whitehead called this stage *Fruition*. Bruce Tuckman labeled it *Performing*.

unknowable future usurp our experience in the present
- Noticing when the past is reaching forward to distort our awareness of the present
- Shutting down our anger so fast we don't even realize it was there
- Letting outrage keep us externally focused
- Being governed by automatic behaviors or reactions
- Slipping into old patterning, learned very early in life to ensure our survival, that leads to familiar, but not necessarily rewarding, outcomes

Each of the above examples shows that something other than our own volition can be in charge of our lives. Something else can stand in authority over us.

A dictator is in charge, but it isn't a man in black at the front of the room. That dictator is riding around under our own skin.

It's Our Own Fight

So much of the time, when we are struggling through the authority phase with someone, we're actually having a fight with ourselves. We're entering a conflict with something inside us.

It's hard to see our own. It's easy to see someone else's.

My friend was outraged when someone helped her navigate a public transit turnstile. Her reaction?

She said to him, "Do you think I can't get through the gate myself?"

Can you see how that is a personal authority issue?

The medium, in this case, was what some of us call a mind read.[3] She placed a thought in his head as the reason for his

---

3 (Agazarian, SCT for Groups 1997) p. 148.

behavior. This thought was seen as a commentary on her abilities.

Her reaction was akin to a child screaming, "I want to do it myself!" I want to be in charge of getting myself through a gate. I don't want anybody else to do it for me. I am the authority on getting myself in and out of a situation.

She's having a fight, but it's her own fight. She is seeing it as a fight with the poor well-meaning stranger who wanted to ease her passage. But he just innocently stepped into her issue. She didn't really see him at all. She needs to prove to herself that she can get herself where she wants to go.

When therapists get together, they sometimes bemoan their heartbreak when a client makes a terrible choice. After awhile in this profession, you can see where paths will lead a client. For years, I couldn't understand why a client would turn away from the road that would lead to her heart's desire and instead choose the turnoff to a virtual slum.

But now I understand. A client would rather be unhappy than surrender authority over his/her own life.

So when her parents and friends are all against her wedding a guy they see as a jerk, she'll defy them, to her own detriment. Because it is her life and her choice and directing her life herself matters more than anything else.

Obviously, oppositional reactions—actions that deliberately oppose family directives or good advice—are just as automatic as blind compliance. A person stuck in opposing others is still not managing his own authority. If you automatically say no when someone offers, you are still being controlled, not by the person who offered, but by the process in you that needs to defy others.

Spiritual Surrender and Authority

When we settle into a spiritual life, we may surrender some of the struggle. But if we have not worked our own authority phase of development, this may not be a clean surrender.

We may not be making important distinctions. Are we surrendering or abdicating? Is our compliance actually avoidance? Are we enrobed by the Spirit or are we in denial? Are we taking responsibility for the choices that are ours alone? Are we using religion to clamp down on feelings we don't want to process? Are we subtly oppositional to other members or the hierarchy.

Traditionally, certain religious groups equated surrender with turning off one's thinking. Don't question. Don't color outside the lines. But we've seen horrific consequences of blind compliance. We know we've been given a brain so that we can use it.

We've been given authority over our one precious life. The challenge is to suss out all the ways our own processes steal that authority from us.

4 THE SHADOW SIDE

Anger! What shall we do with anger?

In the recent past, a split congregation was sent a moderator for a day of reconciliation. His alleged purpose was to bring the two factions together. What do you think would happen if a session began with the following quotes:

But I tell you that anyone who is angry with his brother will be subject to judgment. (Matthew 5:22)

Refrain from anger and turn from wrath; do not fret--it leads only to evil. (Psalm 37:8)

But now you must rid yourselves of all such things as these: anger, rage, malice, slander, and filthy language from your lips. (Colossians 3:8)

Would these verses lead to an honest exchange or would the differences become more entrenched?

At the end of the day, this group's split had widened. The minority became marginalized, and most of these left that church.

They'd been admonished to stifle anger before they even started talking, so they kept their energy captive and that made their own wisdom unavailable to themselves or the group. They could not access all that they knew.

Anger has gotten a bad rap within the church and lots of Christians believe they should never be angry. So what happens then? What happens to the honest energy that is anger?

It has to go somewhere.

Anger will always out. It's like electricity. It's a current that, if not directed, can still burn.

If you've ever been the recipient of passive aggression—and who hasn't—you know it leaves a yucky residue. It's like a stickiness that's hard to wash off. And if it's really subtle, one can feel bad and not know why.

Passive aggression is one of the ways anger short-circuits. Others are rage, outrage, abuse, meanness, negative implying, acting out, acting in, depression, self-harm, self-sabotage, self-victimization, loss of energy, loss of perspective, and irritability. With all these nasty consequences, pure, well-directed anger starts to look like the better option.

The odd thing about indirect or misdirected anger is this, if the anger isn't expressed from the inside, from its actual cause, in a particular way, it never gets satisfied. The extreme example is a serial killer, who tries to kill his mother over and over again. No matter how many victims are slain, it is never enough. The killing has to be reenacted in order to achieve temporary relief from the pressure that is still boiling over.

More common examples are these: the serial gossip, killing reputations right and left; the serial critic, finding fault 24/7; the serial whiner, setting people's teeth on edge; the serial victim, who is happiest when things go wrong and can transform the nicest gesture into a liability. Misdirected anger, all.

Anger, like all feelings, holds a metaphor. The only way to discover it is to make room for the anger in a directed way. Once the metaphor bursts forth, the anger vanishes—and never causes any harm.

But in a community that believes it should stifle anger, appropriate expression of anger is not taught. So it wends its way through one of the more damaging channels.

Men and women are chemically different. That's not news, but one consequence of not recognizing the difference is that girls and women are often trained to handle and suppress anger with the same controls that are taught to boys and young men. Boys are also taught to use catharsis—in physical play, sports, and fighting—as a release for anger, while girls are more often expected to serve and make nice.

Controls that are taught to men aren't necessary for most women. Further, women may stifle their own anger because they've been hurt by angry men, so they put themselves under a mantle that takes the color out of life.

As a therapist, getting women to express anger was one of my greatest challenges. They'd tie themselves in complicated knots to avoid it. They had enormous fears that they wouldn't ever be able to stop being angry or that they'd be destructive. And they were always surprised when they'd use new skills and come to a brand new place of clarity and energy in short order. Their transformation was astonishing, especially given years of locking anger behind a pleasant face.

All feelings, anger included, when handled well, lead to revelations that can't be reached any other way. The creative solution, the energy to carry it out, the heretofore unseen path are all on the other side. Logic won't get you there. Neither will problem solving. In contrast, well-processed feelings pour you into new territory.

But if a community is stifling anger or other emotions, feelings can get stuck. Then the community itself can get stuck. Disappointment, upset over differences, triggers, buried anger— they can all pile up on the shadow side, and they erupt as conflict among the people. Meanwhile, creative revelations are waiting behind the metaphors seeded in the buried anger.

This is the Achilles' heel of the Christian community—

mishandling anger and parish poisons.

In some groups, this is called evil. And if a shadow side gets too much stuff in it for too long, perhaps it does lead to evil choices and terrible harm. But for the ordinary Christian, it's simply a big pit, a basement, with a lot of junk stuck in it, that is polluting the house.

I can hear someone saying, "We know what to do with the shadow side—pray."

Prayer is terrific. Prayer is heavenly. Our connection with God opens doors, no question.

But we also know that miracles are only needed when something is beyond our own resources. Excavating the contents in the basement, sorting through them and putting them where they belong, we can do this. We have the resources. Prayer will grease the skids, of course. But we have our own part.

Like a parent who knows that doing too much for a child will weaken him and keep him from gaining important skills, God has a good sense of when to let us turn to each other for solutions.

5 WHAT'S A BODY TO DO?

The body of Christ has a lot going for it. Most people want to be good. Most people want to be skilled and are willing to learn.

The other good news, on top of the Good News, is that there's a way through to the bright side. Many technical advances have improved our world and this is true in the field of human relations as well.

As I've grown in my profession, I've had the good fortune to study with some of the best therapists and theoreticians of our time, and on the cutting edge today is Dr. Yvonne Agazarian, who has developed a powerful and comprehensive theory of living human systems, complete with an encyclopedic toolbox.

The following statements by Dr. Agazarian undergird the methods that will unfold in this book:

Systems stay stable and survive by integrating similarities. The give-and-take of familiar information between the system and its environment maintains the system in a good relationship with its inner and outer world, keeps the system stable, and increases the probability that it will survive in the short run. Too much similarity and not enough difference, however, introduces redundancy and rigidity, which in the long run will threaten system survival.

Systems close boundaries to differences. Systems have difficulty with differences. Differences introduce new information into the system. Both the new information and the existing system have to be reorganized before the new information can be integrated. Differences create "noise" in the system while the system changes sufficiently to integrate them.

Systems change and transform by integrating differences. The give-and-take of unfamiliar information between the system and its environment require both the system and the environment to develop the ability to change. Differences make for bad relationships within the system and between the system and its environment in the short run, but integrating differences is what enables systems to change and transform in the long run.[4]

Systems are self-correcting. Systems stay stable in the context of an ever-changing world by receiving, containing, and integrating information. Conflictual (noisy) communications destabilize the system. Systems restabilize through conflict resolution, either by splitting off differences that disrupt the existing integration (avoiding change) or by delaying and containing conflict until differences can be integrated.[5]

The process that will unfold in this book is based on these and other systems-centered® principles, offering methods for receiving, containing, and integrating information, and for delaying and containing conflict until differences can be integrated.

Dr. Agazarian's offerings are not limited to theory and practice. She also has boiled down complex, overwhelming behavioral goals into easy-to-learn simple steps.

Scott Peck, in a sermon, once remarked that the beauty of Jesus's message is that it has meaning no matter where you are on the continuum of spiritual growth. The same simple parable can provide guidance to a novice Christian and insight to the experienced follower.

---

[4] (Agazarian, SCT for Groups 1997) p. 19.

[5] Ibid. p. 20.

I've found a similar beauty in Dr. Agazarian's work. From novice to expert, the same simple technique can give blinding discernment.

The organization that tests and teaches her works is the Systems-Centered® Training and Research Institute (SCT®)[6]. Experiencing their methods revolutionized my life and my professional practice. If I had my way, all politicians, world leaders, and bosses would be required to study there.

So much that I will henceforth present has its roots in my training with them. I've seen these methods work in severely fractured groups with very hot collars and inevitably, the new ground discovered is a delight and a surprise, and reverberates in positive ways beyond the immediate and original situation.

It's the most efficient methodology I've ever witnessed.

I will be describing here how to adapt a small sampling of these marvelous processes for use with a church community. The best scenario, by far, would be to import an SCT-trained leader to teach the skills and lead a process with the entire congregation.[7]

The leader training track at SCT takes years, which means that SCT leaders are quite skilled with the subtle shifts in a group that signal the need for intervention—and just what intervention is required at any particular time. SCT leaders are required to spend a goodly portion of those years in authority issue boot camp, so that by the time they survive that, they have been wrung out and re-fluffed inside out.

---

[6] SCT® and Systems-Centered® are registered trademarks of Dr. Yvonne M. Agazarian and the Systems-Centered Training and Research Institute, Inc., a non-profit organization.

[7] Resources can be found at www.systemscentered.com.

If this is beyond possibility, then I emphasize two points regarding leadership and context.

The Leadership Role

First, if you employ the processes described in these chapters, your group must have a leader. The group leader must not be deeply on one side of the split. It would be better if the leader wasn't your own pastor, unless that pastor has been trained by SCT (for some years) and isn't strongly in either faction.

Members of the church hierarchy are not necessarily the best choice. A lay therapist, counselor, or manager trained in group-development processes may well have more up-to-date, concentrated skills that will help them take on the theory and practices described in this book. Thus, someone in the home congregation, as long as they are not too strongly in either camp, may be more effective than clergy in a ranking position.

Even better, have a leadership team; i.e., two people functioning in the leader role. While one leader is directing a process, the other leader can observe the group, noticing what is being dropped, or picking up on subtle signals.

A leader pair can help each other debrief. Leading is a lonely function, and the temptation can be to be drawn to a side. A leader pair gives each leader a subgroup of their own.

I urge both leaders to study this and other recommended books. A later chapter gives additional information about the leader's role.

Context

Second, the processes here are a body of work, meant to be taken together. They are to be used in a particular context.

I'm presenting these techniques for use in the specific context of a split religious community. They are not meant to be translated for use in a professional counseling situation. For that, go to an SCT conference and get the proper guidance and deeper applications for professional therapeutic settings.

Even if a Christian community is functioning well, the process offered here gives a church a way to enhance the skills of the fellowship so that any future conflict already has a built-in method for resolution.

In addition, as members assimilate these skills, their enhanced competence will advance every group experience—Bible study, class participation, and church meetings. This competence will also reverberate beyond the church, giving families tools that they can use at home to strengthen their bonds and become more resilient.

Goal

We can boil the multiple goals of a group down to three:

- To survive
- To develop
- To transform

In a fractured Christian community, survival is the issue, both the survival, on many levels, of the community itself, and the survival of the membership, in the sense that a fractured community starts to lose members. When individual members feel that support for their spiritual life or peace of mind can be met only by leaving, then they depart, taking their energy, talents, tithes, and integrity with them.

When a community gains facility in the skills presented here, they move beyond survival and actually develop as a group, and with continued practice, get to enjoy the heady leap of transformation. (More on this in later chapters.)

The primary approach for reaching these goals is training. The immediate goal for each group meeting will be to learn and practice the skills that further this healing process.

Ultimately, the group will have the capacity to take on the issues that are splitting the community and, using these methods, come to an entirely new resolution that will be funded by energy from both sides. In fact, the sides, by then, will have shifted and the split will turn into a division of tasks.

It will be much more a consensus than a compromise, and as a result of this process, the group as a whole will be tightly bonded.

The Process

Dr. Agazarian has expanded exponentially the body of knowledge about group development. She realized that a group develops in a predictable fashion through a series of predictable issues that bloom in a specific, repeatable order.

It's as if a group climbs a staircase together. While a member or two might be on the third stair and a couple of members might be on the second stair, the bulk of a beginning group will be on the first stair. A group doesn't climb stair 5 and then climb stair 2. Stair 5 is reached after climbing stairs one through four.

Each stair has its own defense. That defense must be decommissioned in order for the group to climb to the next height. So if a group doesn't know how to handle the defense for stair four, it will not comfortably make it to stair six.

A marriage can be stuck for decades on one of the stairs of the authority phase. If the accompanying defense is not dismantled, the couple may never advance. The couple may abdicate certain pieces of their own authority, find a way to keep the peace, be good at an aspect of marriage, such as parenting or finances, but still be very lonely or resigned or stifled. Such a marriage may not be contentious, but it can be quite joyless.

Dr. Agazarian's work includes techniques for dismantling the defenses of each stair-step of the authority (and other) phases. This is why therapists or managers trained by SCT can help their charges to productivity years ahead of traditional group leadership practices. A week at an SCT conference is like the fast lane, skipping hundreds of unproductive detours of traditional and antiquated procedures.

Therapists and consultants generally want the best for their clients and they would like them to achieve solutions as quickly as possible. However, if they lead a client to leap forward to a skill that is—in the SCT system—stair nine, and that client hasn't learned the skills required to climb stairs one through eight, their client's progress will collapse. The person or work-group won't be able to sustain that change. They haven't a sturdy enough foundation.

This same progression is important when bringing a conflicted Christian community through survival to transformation. The skills must be taught in order, one or two at a time, as the group becomes readied to climb the next stair. As tempting as it is to rush forward, especially when there is a lot of pressure to get the church settled down, growth will be lasting only if the congregation really gets comfortable with each set of skills before moving forward.

The stair that handles anger and transforms it into creative energy is a ways up. The skills for the lower stairs must be practiced and become comfortable before the anger skills are tackled.

I have seen individuals, couples, and groups try skipping steps. People might feel better temporarily but the change doesn't go deep enough—without the supporting foundation—to last, and before long, a shiver leads to an earthquake.

The process is worth the reduced velocity. Like Jesus's

message, the simplest beginning skills make a huge difference in the well-being of the individuals and the group as a whole, even as they are building a foundation for the more advanced, higher-stair skills.

Thus, plan for this to take awhile. Slow down. Give the community plenty of time to build its skills. I promise you, in the long run, this process will be brilliantly efficient.

Part 1: Basic Skills

Each member of your church is like a walking gold mine. Beneath the surface they are carrying nuggets of wisdom, experience, and perspective that can greatly benefit your community.

Members can offer their best at Bible study yet stay mute at altar guild. They can offer 24 karat gold at a meeting, book study, task group, or class—or walk out and take it all home.

What makes the difference?

How can every member of your church have enough safety to give each group their best?

The first section of this book offers simple techniques that make a huge difference in the quality of any church gathering. These skills are quickly learned and easily maintained. They provide entry for the quieter members and enough safety for all members to risk their deeper thoughts and experiences.

A church group, no matter how benevolent, is not immune from recognized group dynamics. Churches do have aggressive members and these can unknowingly or, even deliberately, shut down superb offerings from more delicate voices.

Believe it or not, even in a church group, someone will be silently singled out as a scapegoat, unless certain skills are routinely practiced. Think about people in your church. Who do you quietly, subtly, dismiss when they speak?

The following skills guide member communications through a

translucent channel of equity, putting boundaries around the aggressive members and providing pathways for the delicate. They provide a way for members to share their difference of perspective without fearing indirect retaliation (or outright shaming) by more vocal or aggressive members.

By learning and practicing this first set of skills, every church can maximize the contribution of each of its members at every event.

6 Stair-step 1

Becoming a Functional Group

The first task when people come together, especially if they are intending to discuss a mutual problem, is to get all the way there.

When you think about this it makes sense. If we want a group to operate at its highest level, we need all the resources of all the people in the group. Yet this step is often shortchanged. We leave it to individuals to bring themselves into a group. We may think that simply by presenting an agenda or saying a prayer that people are starting in the same place.

But defenses are already operating, even at this very first stair-step. If these defenses are not deliberately weakened, they will push the group off course.

Dr. Agazarian calls this first set social defenses.

"Social defenses are the oil on troubled waters of everyday life. They are the important social skills that allow people to interact socially. Social defenses also constitute a shorthand that signals status in the pecking order and lays down the rules of interpersonal experience."[8]

And what are we defending against when we enter a group? Let's consider this.

---

[8] (Agazarian, SCT for Groups 1997), p. 96.

"Typically, people entering a group greet each other by name, talk about difficulties getting to the group session, tell jokes, catch up on gossip. In short, they are generally disarming and personable. At the same time, each person is sizing up the other members, gauging moods and climate, and locating himself or herself in relation to any new members."[9]

Breaking social rules, says Dr. Agazarian, is such a shaming experience that we first are scoping out what the rules are, watching to see who is one-up or one-down, and making our own statement about where we fit.

Even those who seem to be saying, I don't care about your rules, or I will be as I damn well please, are making a statement that, boiled down, reveals the authority phase. I reject your authority. I am the boss. I am my own boss. I have my own pecking order and all of you are lower. I am my own person, because I am really low on the pecking order. I'm safe because I'm invisible.

One way or the other, we are trying to keep ourselves safe— what a defense is all about.

We may also have some defenses against joining. We don't want to shave even little pieces off ourselves. As much as we may want to belong to a group, we don't want to have to give ourselves up to do it.

Thus the desire to join is offset by the desire to flee. We are poised between joining and flight. Our flight behaviors show when, as the group is trying to form, we do things to pull attention to the outside of the group. Interrupting, making a announcement that relates to something other than the group's immediate business,

---

[9] (Agazarian, SCT for Groups 1997), p. 97.

running out to go to the bathroom at the last minute, resisting sitting in the circle, staying too long in a private conversation with someone else in a corner, staying in the kitchen to wash one last dish or check the biscuits one more time, requiring a leader or other member to call you again by name.

True member behavior means being in your seat fully ready before the time boundary is crossed, something you see in a high-functioning, well-trained group.

The second time you meet—and at all meetings thereafter—you will modify this defense by centering. The first time you meet, the group must learn an important skill, the bread and butter of turning a stereotypical group into a high functioning, creative group.

Skill—Functional Subgrouping[10]

Groups typically split over differences and stereotype those in the opposite camp. Functional subgrouping offers an alternative to the usual course by deliberately containing differences in separate subgroups that then explore their side of the issue.

"Functional subgrouping is the conflict resolution method of containing conflict through the change process until differences in the apparently similar are recognized and similarities in the apparently different can be discovered and integrated."[11]

This skill appears to be so simple, it seems easy. Experience a group using it, versus a group not using it, and its brilliance starts to show. The more a group is held to the structure of using it, the faster it will advance.

------

[10] This technique was developed by Yvonne Agazarian and is basic to all SCT groups. It is described and the foundational theory fully explained in *Systems-Centered Therapy for Groups*, pp. 44-83.

[11] Ibid, p. 20.

It is your number one weapon against stereotypical group behavior, rejecting differences, scapegoating, and marginalizing members who are too different. It makes possible the integration of differences and enables a group to handle increasingly complex issues.

"The first rule of subgrouping is to join with those who have a similar experience."[12] "The art of subgrouping is keeping communication balanced, that is, putting into one's side of the scale a balancing communication of equal or slightly more weight than the communication one has just received."[13]

Three, sometimes four, steps are involved.

1. **Invitation**. At the end of a statement or comment, the speaker adds, "Anybody else?"[14] [15]

2. **Join**. The next person begins her/his statement by joining to something in the previous speaker's comment. She/He starts her/his comment by finding a personal similarity to the previous comment. The join must be genuine, not a disguised 'yes-but.'

3. **Build**. Then the 2nd person builds on the similarity, adding a bit that is their own exploration, and ending with an invitation for the next join.[16]

Example—Clean Subgrouping:

Speaker A, "That steeple has been there since the church was

---

[12] (Agazarian, SCT for Groups 1997), p. 60.

[13] (Agazarian, SCT for Groups 1997), p. 55.

[14] (Agazarian, SCT for Groups 1997), p. 44.

[15] (Agazarian, Approach 2001), p. 108.

[16] (Agazarian, SCT for Groups 1997), p. 45.

built. I don't see any reason to change it just because the Methodists got a new steeple. Anybody else?" [Invitation]

Speaker B, "I join A on not wanting to change the steeple. [Join] I like it the way it is. I can see it from my house and I'm inspired by it. [Build] **Anybody else?**"

Speaker C, "I **join** B on being inspired by the steeple. It's a spire. Spire comes from spirit. Being inspired means filling with spirit. A steeple gives inspiration. Our steeple reminds me to look up. [Build] Loping it off would be a travesty. **Anybody else?**"

Speaker D, "I **join** C on the idea of travesty. I feel a loss at the very thought of shortening the steeple. [Build] **Anybody else?**"

In the above example, everyone followed the process. By doing so, they became a subgroup, the subgroup of members who care about keeping the steeple as it is.

Subgrouping in this way is a powerful tool. It's different from subgrouping according to external or superficial characteristics such as age, gender, or church rank. Anyone who has a similarity on this aspect of the issue can be a member.

When a group gets skilled in functional subgrouping, members start to trust that they'll never have to work alone. They can risk climbing out on a limb, because they can trust that someone will climb out there with them. This opens the group to explore the unknown, which is where the answers are.

After all, if the answer were known, there wouldn't be a problem. Only when a group is safe to explore will it venture into new territory.

As simple as this seems, there are lots of ways to subgroup incorrectly.

Example—Unskilled Subgrouping

See if you can spot any mistakes in the following example.

Speaker E, "I don't see the purpose of a steeple. All the heat rises into it and nobody is ever up there. It's a waste of electricity. Anybody else?"

Speaker F, "Speaking of waste, we should change our garbage service. They left cups all over the ground. Anybody else?"

Speaker G, "I agree with E. A steeple is superfluous. The Holy Risers don't have a steeple and they have ten times the members as we do. We need money. We need more...."

Speaker H, "Money is the wrong problem. Money is dirty. We shouldn't even be thinking of money at a time like this. Anybody else?"

Speaker I, "Money is a problem for many people, and the steeple is already there, so it would take money to get rid of it. I think we should keep the steeple as is."

Skill Practice

What contrast did you notice between the two subgroups? It could be interesting to use this as an exercise on subgrouping. Using the three steps of functional subgrouping, discuss the differences between the two examples. Give it 5 minutes.

Subgrouping mistakes in the unskilled example:

- Speaker F joined only to a word in E's comment, not to the message, and thereby changed the subject.
- Speaker G used the word agree, which is a different process from joining on a similarity. This is a common mistake in new subgroups and the leader must intervene each time (What is your join?) or the group will move toward their heads and away from their hearts. The organic solution will be bypassed.
- Speaker G joined, not to the previous speaker, but to

someone earlier in the chain. Granted, F didn't give much to join to. It would take some talent to come up with a true join that furthered the subgroup. Waste would be an entry; i.e., "I join on not wanting waste as well. If we repair the steeple, we waste resources we need for more important things, like striping the parking lot. Anybody else?"

- Speaker H interrupted G, not waiting for the anybody else?
- Speaker I did a yes-but. He's really for the steeple and belongs in the other subgroup.

The Active Listening Step

A remedy for a group that is not catching on to joining is to add a step between 1 and 2.

1. **Invitation**. At the end of a statement or comment, the speaker adds, "Anybody else?"
2. **Active Listening**. Before the next person joins, he/she repeats the essence of the speaker's comment.
3. **Join**. When the listener gets it right, she then begins with her join to a similarity in that speaker's comment.
4. **Build**. Then the listener builds on the similarity, adding a bit that is their own exploration.

Example— Subgrouping with Active Listening

Speaker E, "I don't see the purpose of a steeple. All the heat rises into it and nobody is ever up there. It's a waste of electricity. Anybody else?"

Speaker F, "You don't see the point of a steeple. You think a steeple wastes electricity. [Active Listening] I don't like waste. [Kind of a join] And I don't like waste in the parking lot either. Anybody else?"

Speaker G, "I agree with E. A steeple is superfluous."

Leader, *"What did you hear Speaker F say?"*

Speaker G, "He doesn't like waste. And he wants to change the garbage service."

Leader, *"Yes. What similarity can you join to, that relates to the steeple, which is the current topic?"*

Speaker G, "I don't think the steeple is important. [Join] The Holy Risers don't have a steeple and they have ten times the members as we do. We need money. We need …"

Speaker H, "Money is the wrong…"

Leader. *"Speaker H, can you hold for a moment? G hasn't said anybody else."*

Speaker H, "Oh. OK."

Speaker G, "[Build] Our income is down. We need more members so that we have more money. And we can't afford to do anything to the steeple. Anybody else?"

Speaker H, "Money is the wrong problem."

Leader, *"Speaker H. First tell us the gist of Speaker G's comment."*

Speaker H, "She's concerned about our cash flow and she thinks this whole steeple business isn't important."

Leader, to G, *"Is that close enough?"*

G nods.

Leader, to H, *"Good. What is your similarity?"*

Speaker H, "Money is dirty. We shouldn't even be thinking of money at a time like this. Anybody else?"

Speaker I, "Money is a problem for many people, and the steeple is already there…"

Leader, *"First, Speaker I, relate the essence of what H said."*

Speaker I, "He thinks we should be above concerns about money. He doesn't like talking about money."

Leader, to H, *"Close enough?"*

Speaker H, "He said it better than I did."

Leader, to I, *"You bought the right to speak."*

Speaker I, "Since the steeple is already there, and it would take money to get rid of it. I think we should keep the steeple as is."

Leader, *"So you're actually in the other subgroup."*

Speaker I, "I guess I am."

Leader, *"Who has a join to Speaker H?"*

Silence. Which may mean the subgroup is done, or that the dirty money comment is too much difference for the anti-steeple subgroup.

Leader, *"Is this subgroup done with its exploration for now?"*

Did you detect a difference in the group when members were held to the discipline of active listening before adding their join? After all, you can't find a similarity in a person's comment if you haven't been listening.

FAQ

Q. Anybody else? How can such a short phrase be so important?

A. You're forgiven. I'm here. I love you. I've got your back. I'm sorry. It's a girl.

Q. What is the function of the *Anybody else?*

A. *Anybody else* does two things.

- It signals that you are through talking.
- It invites another person to join you.

This keeps the group vectored toward a path of similarities.

Q. If the opposing groups don't talk to each other, how does anything get done?

A. How much gets done when groups are in opposition? Generally they try to convince each other, get more entrenched, build bigger defenses and more complicated strategies. We'll get to how things get done. First we're simply teaching a group how to reach its highest functionality.

Principles

- Opposing subgroups never work with each other.
- Opposing viewpoints always work in separate subgroups.
- The appropriate response to an 'Anybody else?' is a join. Members are to respond with a similarity.
- A member of a subgroup is never dropped. Group members are charged to find some way to join.
- If the leader intervenes to stop the work of the subgroup—time for a break or the other subgroup—she must include an active listening comment that validates the last speaker's message since she prevented a join.
- Joins should be quick. Members are to jump in, or the group will get slower and slower and there will be long silences.
- Comments should be brief, not long monologues, or the group will lose energy and members will get lost as to where to join. (The beauty of subgrouping is that one person isn't responsible for coming up with the great idea. By building on each other's thoughts, the great idea will emerge.)
- A subgroup does not have to confine itself to a narrow topic or even its stance. As it works and defenses lower, the doors to the unknown begin opening. The comments will evolve as the group oozes into the unknown and finds new ideas.

Slowing Down

There's a lot to learn to become a well-trained, functional group and taking the time to become proficient at functional subgrouping is worth the investment. Functional subgrouping is a tool used at every stage, every stair-step.

Functional subgrouping gives energy to a group, and at some point it will want to race off and leave subgrouping behind. The leader's job is to continue to help the group with the discipline, inserting 'anybody else' every single time an excited member forgets.

The leader also has to keep a sharp eye on whether a join is true or not, to protect the work of the subgroup in play. A subgroup will eventually exhaust the available aspects of its topic and the other subgroup will then get a chance to work.

When a subgroup starts repeating itself or runs out of steam, the leader can ask, "Are you ready for the other subgroup to work?" or "Can you hold and let the other subgroup go?" With an affirmative, the leader looks around the circle and asks, "Who has energy to start a different exploration?"

And the opposing subgroup begins.

Differences

Question: How are differences handled?

Answer: Someone says, "I have a difference."

This can be the kickoff for a different subgroup to form and to explore an opposing viewpoint. Also, a person within a subgroup can realize their opinion falls more in line with the other subgroup and then will drop out of the first group's exploration.

Example—Skilled Handling of a Difference

Speaker J, "In this economy, spending money to maintain the steeple, when there are so many other important concerns, doesn't feel right to me. Anybody else?"

Speaker K, "I join J on an awareness of other concerns. I'm

thinking of the mold in the children's building. It isn't good for kids to breathe that. I realize I'm getting off topic, so I'll just say, money is a way we indicate our priorities. My priority is the people, not the structure. Anybody else?"

Speaker L, "I join on the idea of my priority being people rather than structures, but I'm also aware that the steeple is more than a structure—it's a metaphor. It can be seen all over town. Oh, I have a difference! I'm transferring to the other subgroup. Anybody else?"

Leader, "The subgroup can either find a similarity in L's comment or go back to K's and join K."

Speaker M, "I join L on my priority being people rather than structures. We want to model and actually be, the best Christians we can be. And that means, to me, that we put our resources into the needs of people. Anybody else?"

As you can see from the example, clean subgrouping leads to revelation, both for the group and the individual. Members find themselves in new territory. The process becomes so exciting that the old entrenched positions fall away as members make discoveries.

FAQ

Q. Can a person be in two subgroups?

A. Not at the same time. A person can only work in one subgroup at a time.

Q. Does a person have to stay in a subgroup?

A. No. Membership is fluid. When a member becomes aware of having a difference [or the leader detects that a comment is a difference], the leader or the member looks at how great the difference is. If it is much more in alignment with the other subgroup, the member should shift. If it is a just noticeable difference, part of the evolution of the subgroup's work, it is appropriate for the member to stay with the working subgroup.

Q. Are people shifting their seats when they change subgroups?

A. No. Everyone stays in their own seat. As subgroups advance in their work, members switch subgroups a lot.

Q. How do you keep track of who's in whose subgroup?

A. Anyone can ask, "Who's in this subgroup?" Subgroup members then raise their hands.

Handing off

Subgroups take turns working, each subgroup working for awhile, then making room for the other subgroup to work. The leader can direct this, but members can also say, "I really have a difference and I want our subgroup to work now."

However, members are asked to develop attunement, to notice when a subgroup has a lot of energy for its work and is getting somewhere, to not interrupt when that creative energy is flowing.

When the next subgroup takes the floor, the newly silent subgroup maintains roving eye contact within its own group. This keeps the group linked until it's time for its next round of exploration.

Contrast to Stereotypical Groups

Two volunteers are found in nearly every stereotypical group, even in Christian groups which (usually) try hard to be loving. Sometimes the individual member volunteers for one of these positions, sometimes the group elects someone. This is done nonverbally.

The scapegoat position is where the group dumps feelings it doesn't want, and like the goat in the Old Testament that was used to contain the community's hatred, the scapegoat in the group is used to hold the group's anger and ill feelings. Sometimes a person will draw scapegoating to himself by being too different or by broadcasting victim energy.

The identified patient volunteers by drawing the group's focus to his/her ailments or physical problems. That person holds the wounded or disabled energy for the group and offers the group a focus for caretaking. Giving energy is sent to that person, an object for generosity and care.

Groups select these containers quite unconsciously and those who volunteer for the positions may also be doing so unconsciously. The identified patient is not necessarily the sickest or most disabled person in the group, but someone who early in the process calls for care or attention for her/his problems.

Neither position gets much traction in a group with functional subgrouping if the leader is paying attention to the emergence of the roles. If someone starts to be scapegoated, the leader either joins or asks for a join. Thus the group is taught to contain its own negative energy. If someone starts to be seen or to volunteer as the identified patient, the leader lifts up the longing to be taken care of and sends that subgroup into an exploration.

The Silent Members

In nearly every group, a few members don't participate in either subgroup. These are the silent members and there is always a reason. Usually, silent members are holding something for the group, and what they hold is often valuable.

Here is another way SCT techniques are a departure from traditional groups. In most groups, the silent members walk out the door at the end of the meeting, taking their little gold nuggets with them. The system then loses a potential treasure.

At some point, after both subgroups have done some work, before a break, or when a leader is sensing a pulsing gold nugget, the leader asks, *"What are the silent members holding?"*

Speaker N, "I don't belong in either subgroup. I think we should have two steeples. Anybody else?"

Speaker O. "I join on not belonging in either subgroup. I'm thinking about how our steeple is a message to the town. Everyone can see it. It's a witness. And if it deteriorates or if it's maintained, it is still a witness, and with either message, as a stressed steeple or as a freshly painted steeple, it calls out. Anybody else?"

Anne Katherine

7 Crossing the Boundary

People walk in with their social defenses in play. Certain structures then define a clear boundary between group and not-group. Setting these structures and moving quickly into functional subgrouping helps the members cross the boundary.

Structure 1— Physical arrangement

Chairs should be arranged in a single circle, no tables within the circle. Expand the circumference to accommodate the size of the group so that there is no inner or outer circle. It is better to have a giant unwieldy circle than inner and outer.

Once people are seated, ask them to arrange their chairs so that they can see each other. They will shift and check that they have eye contact all around. This weakens the defense of hiding (for the person who wants to back their chair out a bit so they are sort of out of the group) and blocking (for the person who wants to sit a bit forward of everyone). An experienced group will do this automatically and won't have to be reminded.

Structure 2—Time boundaries

Start the group exactly on time and end on time. Observe the difference between groups that start on time and those who don't. Notice which is the cleaner, more productive group.

There's a security that grows when people can count on exactly how much will be asked of them in terms of time and energy. Punctual people are rewarded and latecomers will have to bring

49

themselves in. It's best not to give a review to those who are late. A few words like, "At the break, you can check to see what we've already covered," signals them that catching up is their own responsibility.

A group that waits for everyone to arrive gives authority to latecomers and the group will start later and later. People will learn they can squeeze in another something before leaving for the group and you will be starting without all your resources.

Tool—Guided Centering

The first task before a group can work is to help everyone be as present as they can get. This is a two-part process and the first part is guided centering.

Many Christian communities start things off with a prayer, and this can be added before centering. To avoid a prayer that slants the group toward the bias of the person praying, use one of the following. Even a standardized prayer can subtly direct the group to not be angry or to submit to authority.

Opening Prayers

Prayer A.

Father God, Lord Jesus,

We come together here with the desire to find our way through an issue that matters to us. We ask you to bless our efforts and to help us open to our own wisdom and the wisdom of others.

Thank you for this opportunity.

Amen.

Prayer B.

Holy God, Christ Jesus,

We offer ourselves to the work of our community. We carry an intention to be genuine, as honest as possible, and open to wise guidance both from our own inner spirit, the spirit of our leader, and the Holy Spirit.

Thank you in advance for the blessing of this work.

Amen.

Prayer C.

Open our hearts and our minds, Lord. Help us to see, hear, and feel. Thank you for the gift of this community. Be with us in our work.

Amen.

(If the leader uses a prayer from this chapter, and changes it to subtly influence the group, pay attention. Figure out how you've been influenced and speak up. At the end of your comment say, "Anybody else?")

Even with a good prayer, you aren't done. While we may very much want to belong, another aspect of ourselves wants to be independent. Most of us have some resistance as we enter a group. Our defense against joining is likely to be humming.

If this defense is ignored, the individuals, and the group as well, will carry split attention. Partly they are here. But their minds are also in the car, at home, working, dreaming, planning.

Thus, after the first group meeting, where everyone has learned functional subgrouping, all sessions start with guided centering.

Guided centering begins with an instruction on posture, as you'll see in the examples below. Groups work better when individuals have both feet on the floor, their spines in alignment, and they are sitting erect rather than slouching. We want energy to be directed toward the work of the group, not leaking out due to a slouch or being discharged through fidgets.

The leader leads guided centering, speaking a bit slower than usual with brief pauses between directions. (No long silences.) Give people time to follow the leader's instructions. Once the group has learned to handle anger productively, group members can take a turn at being the leader for centering.

Guided Centering A

Let's center. Place both feet on the floor, spine in alignment, arms comfortably resting, eyes closed.

Slowly rock your feet forward and back. Put all your attention on your feet. Never push too far. Never hurt yourself.

Simply sink into the rhythm of rocking your feet, forward and back. Slowly.

[pause]

Notice how far up your legs that sensation goes.

[pause]

To your calves?

[pause]

To your knees?

[pause]

How far?

[pause]

Very slowly, bring your feet to a rest.

[pause]

What happens to the sensation?

[pause]

Do you still feel energy in your legs.

[pause]

How far up your legs does that energy go?

[pause]

Let your attention travel up your legs...

Through your trunk, your belly...

To your chest, all the way to your head.

[pause]

Slowly lean your head toward your shoulder.

[pause]

Never push. Never hurt.

[pause]

Then slowly lean your head toward your other shoulder. Stop at whatever position feels comfortable, hold...

Then slowly bring it back to the other shoulder.

[pause]

Follow that rhythm back and forth.

[From here forward, the pauses are left out, but continue to pause between directions so that the pace is slow.]

How far away does that experience travel?

To your shoulders? Down your arms?

Very slowly, bring your head back to center. Notice, is there still energy in your neck? How far down does that energy go?

Let your attention sink to your hands. Very slowly, never pushing, never straining, flex your wrists so that your hands move upward in the direction of your shoulders.

Then, slowly, move your wrists so that your hands point downward.

Very slowly, follow the rhythm of your hands flexing up and down.

What other muscles get involved?

How far does the energy travel?

Very slowly, bring your hands to a rest. How far does the energy still go?

See if you can connect the hand energy with the neck energy. See if you can connect the upper energy with the leg energy. Where do they meet?

Notice the rhythm of your breathing.   Notice the filling as you bring air in. Feel how you make space inside yourself for your breath. How much space do you make?

Notice what happens as you release your breath. You are letting your breath go. You are letting go.

See how much you can notice about that rhythm between filling and releasing.

Filling.

And releasing.

Notice two more.

Filling.

And releasing.

Filling.

Releasing.

At your next filling, take your attention to the very bottom of the breath.

Keep your attention there as you release the next breath. Is that your center?

Hang out for a moment and notice what it's like to just be in that place inside of you. Take whatever time you need to find your center.

Notice.

You don't have to do anything. Simply notice what's going on there.

When you are ready, let your awareness expand, growing out from that center.

Let your awareness expand to this context, this room, this group.

You might be ready to open your eyes and when you do, let yourself look lightly, in a soft focus, around the circle. Let go of any need to be social. Simply let your eyes travel slowly around the circle, softly focused, gently taking in each face and moving on to the next.

When you have crossed the boundary into the group and are more present, say, "I'm here."

Guided Centering B

Let's center. Place both feet on the floor, spine in alignment, arms comfortably resting, eyes closed.

Let's move from outside ourselves to inside ourselves. Notice your skin. Notice the temperature of the air on your skin, the feel of your clothing.

[pause]

Do your sleeves feel different to your skin than your shoes?

Notice your points of contact with other objects, the chair, the floor.

[pause]

Do you feel a difference in temperatures?

[pause]

Is warmth coming from one direction and coolness from another?

[pause]

Gradually move your attention through your skin to your muscles. Is there a difference between some muscles and others?

[pause]

Are some relaxed and others carrying tension?

[pause]

You don't have to do anything about this. Just notice.

[pause]

Let your attention sink down to your bones.

[pause]

Imagine the lowest bone of your spine, and then of the next

bone on top of that one, and the next bone on top of that one, so you are piling each spine bone on top of the one below it.

[pause]

Build your column on up, slowly, to your neck.

[pause]

Your lower neck bone sitting on your spine bone.

[pause]

And the next neck bone sitting on the first neck bone.

[pause]

And then your head is sitting on your neck bone.

[pause]

And at the very top of your head is a golden thread. That golden thread comes down from the Creator and down through your neck and into your heart.

[pause]

The gold light fills your heart. Your heart is full of light.

[Continue pausing between each direction.]

And the light spreads into your chest and your chest is full of light.

And the light expands from your chest through your shoulders. And your shoulders are full of light and the light sinks down your arms until your hands are holding light.

And your head is full of light and the light sinks down through your body, through your legs to your feet and your feet are full of light and you are standing in light.

And your attention is rooted in your center, which is full of light. You settle into your center, your light-filled center.

Take all the time you want, resting in your center.

And when you are ready, let your awareness expand, still rooted in your light-filled center.

Let your awareness expand to this context, this room, this

group.

You might be ready to open your eyes and when you do, let yourself look lightly, in a soft focus, around the circle. Let go of any need to be social. Simply let your eyes travel slowly around the circle, softly focused, gently taking in each face and moving on to the next.

When you have crossed the boundary into the group and are more present, say, "I'm here."

8 STAIR 1—GETTING ALL THE WAY PRESENT

One more tool will be used to help the group members become completely present. This will be introduced at the third session.

"What?" You say. "We're still on Stair 1?"

Yes, we are almost on the other side of the social defenses, and some people may still have one foot in and one foot out of the group. Some people may be distracted.

A distraction is something that is keeping someone's energy from being all the way present in the group. Again, our goal is to have a group with full access to the resources of each member, and if someone's attention is split, their resources are not fully available to the group.

Even though it is taking three chapters to get feet fully planted on stair 1, in reality, once a group is used to this progression, these first tools may take no more than five to ten minutes, a good investment of time when you consider that you then have a fully present group ready and available for work.

After centering, after everyone says, "I'm here," the leader asks, *"Is anyone distracted?"*

Members who are aware of being distracted then voice this or raise their hands.

Leader: *"Who is willing or has energy to go first to work with their distraction?"*

Skill. Handling a Distraction[17]

1. The leader instructs, *"State the facts first, the feelings second?"* If feelings are mixed up in the member's statement, the leader counsels, *"Slow down. What are the facts?"*

> **Distraction Exercise, Part 1**
>
> L. *State the facts of your distraction first and the feelings second.*
>
> M. My husband took my car and that's why I was late and I'm really upset, because. . .
>
> L. *Slow down. State the facts first.*

2. After the person lists the facts, the leader then asks, *"How do you feel about the facts?"*

> **Distraction Exercise, Parts 2 and 3.**
>
> L. *How do you feel about the facts, for example, the fact that your husband took your car today?*
>
> M. I was okay with that. I knew he was going to.
>
> L. *What are your feelings about the fact that he was late getting back?*
>
> M. Irritated, frustrated, angry. Stuck!
>
> L. *What about the fact he was late because he picked up the cat's medicine?*
>
> M. Grateful. Relieved. We can get her treatment started.

3. If the member needs more guidance, the leader asks for the feelings connected to each fact. Some members are helped if the leader re-states the facts or asks for the feelings for each fact one at a time.

---

[17] This tool was designed and developed by Yvonne Agazarian and SCT. For the entire process, see *Systems-Centered Therapy for Groups*, pp. 75-79.

4. Next the feelings are brought across the boundary into the
    group. *"Bring your*

Distraction Exercise, Part 4.

L. Bring your feelings into the group by making eye contact with each member around the circle.

feelings into your relationship with each person."

By bringing her feelings *into* the group, rather than trying to keep a part of herself out, a member can be much more available. The leader instructs members to simply return eye contact, making every effort to not insert a social response. The goal is to help contain the feelings.

5. Verify that the exercise worked: *"Check in with yourself and see if your energy is more in the group, less in the group, or the same."* [18]

    After the person has made eye contact with each person, the leader verifies that the exercise worked to bring the person more into the group.

    If the member is the same or less present, he/she probably has another distraction. The leader can continue with that person, or go on to another distracted person and come back if it's still necessary. *[I'm going to work with L's distraction and then I'll check back with you.]*

Judgment Call

The leader must discern whether a distraction is just a distraction or is work for the group. For example, if the distraction is about something Person A said to Person B right before group started, it might well be work for the group. In that case, the leader says so, and asks if the person can hold until all the distractions are

---

[18] (Agazarian, SCT for Groups 1997), p. 79.

handled.

Sometimes lots of people will have distractions, and the leader will patiently lead each person through the exercise. Often, reducing distractions for one or two people brings even the others into the group and their distractions fade away.

If half the group time is spent reducing distractions, that's okay. The exercise is teaching the whole group to separate feelings from facts, useful in any case. The group may also be reluctant to begin work, so the pull to the outside is enhanced. In the flight subphase, taking the time for distractions helps contain this energy until the group is ready.

The leader will have to deal with her own internal push to get the task done. The priority is always to get the whole group present first, in order for all resources to be available for the work of the group.

One of the interesting aspects of this type of group process is this: members who are observing rather than actively participating are still 'working along.' Since defenses are lowering for the entire group with almost every intervention, their personal resources are ever more freed to work silently along while another group member or subgroup is active. Hence issues—and skills—move forward even for observing members.

A similar thing happens when new members, who haven't had the benefit of the first learning-intensive sessions, join. The progress of the more experienced members is observed and modeled after by the new members. At the entry of all new members, the basic three-step of functional subgrouping is introduced, but then the group is allowed to take off at its current level of development.

Hence, experienced members are rewarded for their seniority, rather than forced to sit through boring replays ad infinitum.

Sometimes a person will be more here, but not all the way here, after undoing their distractions. That's good enough. The idea is to get as here as possible. If they have a big thing going on elsewhere in their lives, even a little more here is helpful.

FAQ

Q. It takes three sessions before the group can get to a task? That's a lot of time.

A. It doesn't have to be. The first three sessions can occur in a morning or at one event. A possible two and a half hour (if time boundaries are kept) structure is as follows:

~ Session 1. (40 minutes)

~ Introduce subgrouping skill.

~ Skill practice using contrast between the two sample groups in chapter as exercise.

~ Practice subgrouping with a mild decision, such as:

  o Should people early to church park in the further part of the parking lot?

  o Should the church picnic be at a park or at the church?

  o Does it matter to thank people who give service to the church—like ushers, heads of committees, lectors, volunteer cooks.

~ Introduce Surprises and Learnings

~ Break (5 minutes)

~ Session 2. (40 minutes)

~ Introduce centering.

~ Subgrouping skill practice using low-heat topic.

  o Is it better for the choir to take communion at beginning or end of rest of congregation?

  o Do we care if priests receive their Eucharist before or

after rest of congregation?

- o Should we have separate times for prey and predators at the animal blessing?
- o Do we want to landscape exterior spaces so that yard maintenance does not require gasoline or electricity?
~ Surprises and Learnings.
~ Break (5 minutes)
~ Session 3. (50 minutes)
~ Theory (5 minutes)
- o An illustrated diagram of subgrouping and energy boundaries
    - ▪ YouTube video
~ Center
~ Introduce Distraction Exercise
~ Subgrouping skill practice using mild-heat topic.
- o Do we need to provide offering envelopes?
- o Shall we use the hymnals for services or put all the hymns in the church bulletin?
~ Surprises and Learnings

Surprises and Learnings[19]

Each session, and sometimes each skill practice, ends with the leaders asking people to share their surprises, learnings, satisfactions, dissatisfactions, or discoveries.

This practice has two benefits. It creates a space for each person to apply the previous work to their own lives, to give themselves a take home message. It also signals the transition from group to non-group.

---

[19] (Agazarian, SCT for Groups 1997) p. 226.

An *anybody else* is not required here, but a well-trained group will say it anyway. In this case, the next member joins not to the content but to the sharing of a surprise or learning, etc.

9 THE GROUP-AS-A-WHOLE

All members are part of the group-as-a-whole. Members (M) join subgroups as they find that they carry a similarity with whatever aspect of an issue that subgroup is working.

The two grayer members are silent members, not yet working in a subgroup.

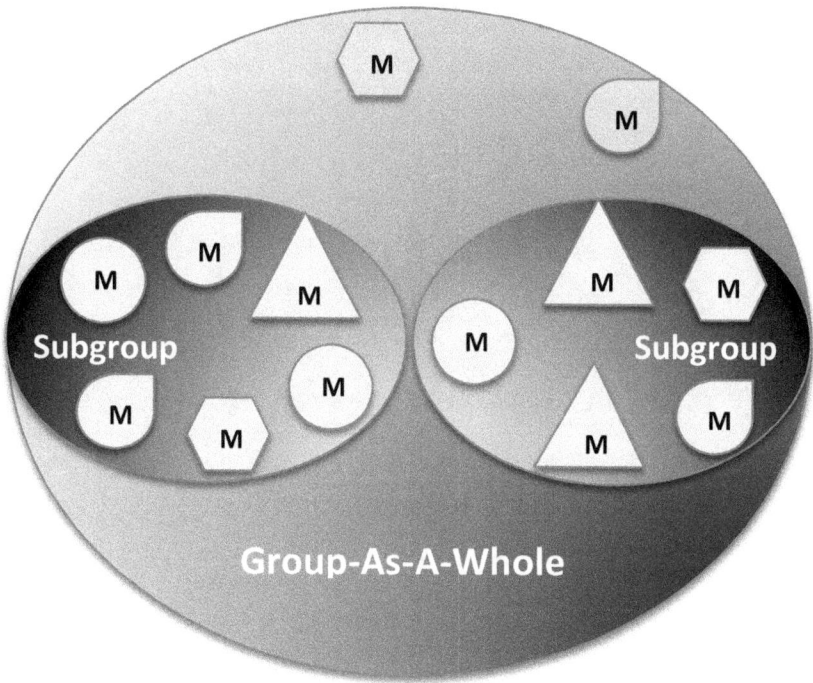

As each subgroup works, members will begin to discover that they have similarities with members in the other subgroup and the populations will shift.

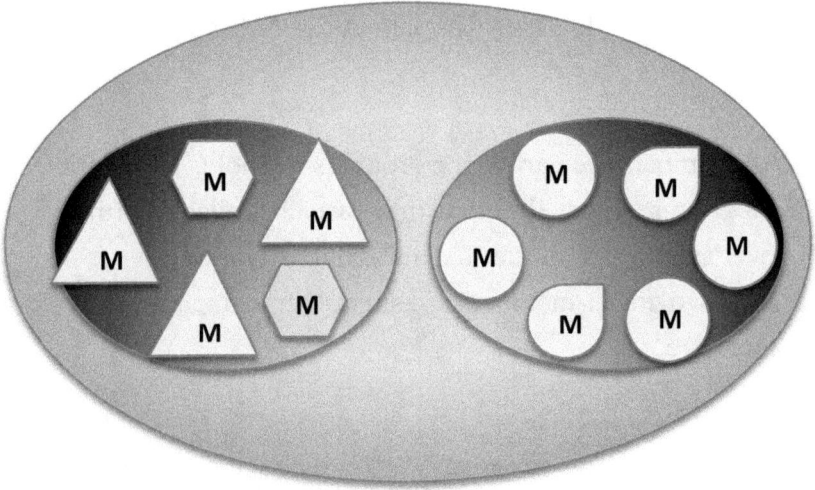

10 TITRATING THE TASK

A group based on SCT principles carries two agendas:
- To become a more functional group
- To do whatever task is before it

The leader, therefore, is presiding over both. Her primary attention, especially at first, is training the group in the skills that will make a difference forever. The more skilled the group becomes, the more elegant will be the solutions and processes the group undertakes.

On its way to proficiency, tasks for the group should be titrated or adjusted, so that it is handling issues commensurate with its skill level.

Therefore, even if, or especially if, there is a large, hot issue that the parish is facing, the group as a whole will do better if it waits to confront that issue until after it is subgrouping easily. Once the group is proficient through the fifth stair-step, then the issue can be brought to the group. It will have the foundation and the discipline to deal with it.

If a parish knows it is heading for a difficult or complex issue, it helps if everyone understands that although that task is before them, getting all the way through the task will take some weeks, or even some months, depending how often the group is meeting, so that they can learn to use the tools that will help them to a much more unified, elegant solution.

A group has a lot to learn at first and we want to keep the goal of skill enhancement in view. It can still move into a task, even at the first session, but the primary goal for beginning sessions is for the group to get their toolbox set up.

Time will be made up at the other end. Once the group is proficient and has more experience, it will get through tasks beautifully and quickly.

A church group always has a lot to decide, so one of the tasks of the early group, while it is still learning to climb the staircase, could be to list all the issues and rank them according to difficulty or heat.

Doing vs. Becoming

There are two types of groups:

- Task groups
- Process groups.

A task group gets together to get something done—plan a budget, line up adult education, study a scripture. A task group usually functions better if a member takes on the job of scribe, listing the group's ideas on a board or paper so that the group stays organized as to topic.

A process group gets together to move through something—a conflict, an advent meditation, a spiritual exercise.

In either case, functional subgrouping is the fast lane to energetic group participation and forward movement.

A congregation trained in functional subgrouping and defense modification can use these skills for almost every get-together.

Recently I was at an advent workshop. I could tell the leader was trying hard to pull the group into more active participation, and she even spontaneously used the phrase, "Anybody else?" after each person spoke, although I don't think she has had SCT training.

The group wanted to be cooperative. I felt no resistance in the group, other than the natural defenses of stairs 1 and 2. Someone would speak and then there'd be a silence, not just of contemplation, but of holding back.

And I thought how different and exciting the group would have been if they'd had the simple structure of functional subgrouping to give them a way to interact.

At one point, a member deepened the group from the head to the heart by her genuine sharing. Then another member shared something very touching. Many of us had tears in a join with her. She started apologizing for being so emotional, but she was not at all being out of line or too much. I thought, here's a case of having gone out on the limb and feeling alone out there. It was a genuine sharing but then I think it started feeling to her like too much of a risk.

Functional subgrouping would have saved her from that. This was an example of a group moving higher on the staircase without the skills to support that advance.

11 STAIR 2—DEFENDING USING THOUGHTS

Really? After all this, we're only at Stair 2?

Yes.

What's your hurry?

We become more aware of our 'hurry up' culture in a group using SCT skills. We notice our internal pressure to get the job done. We want to give short shrift to these piddling little interferences like centering or reducing distractions. Then we're surprised at the speed with which the actual meat of the session is accomplished, thanks to those piddling initial tasks.

My experience with stair climbing is that after a defense—such as a social defense—is modified, the group leaps forward, gets somewhere, has some energy, and then suddenly runs into the next riser.

The new defense has arrived. If it is handled, the group leaps forward with a new spurt of energy and gets further. And eventually the group runs into the next new riser, challenged to weaken the newly arrived defenses.

Thoughts that Defend Us Against Feelings

Stair 2 invites the group to test reality and to discover the difference between explaining and exploring. The defenses that signal arrival at Stair 2 are called cognitive defenses.[20] The harbinger of a cognitive defense is anxiety or worry.

Cognitive defenses are frightening or upsetting thoughts that are a defense against something going on in the present. "Cognitive defenses enable the individual to avoid the conflicts in the here-and-now."[21] These thoughts seem real, but they are actually just thoughts. And although they are being employed to protect us from something, they often cause more trouble than whatever is hidden behind them.

By testing reality, we shrink the frightening thought and find out what it is we are hiding from.

Thoughts can be grouped according to the following:
- Thoughts about the future (sometimes influenced by thoughts from the past).
- Thoughts about what other people are thinking.
- Thoughts about the unknown.

Each type of thought has a simple technique to test the reality of what the thought is presenting, and then finishes with a way to find out what was defended against.

Each technique has three parts:
- Reality test
- Curiosity
- Verifying or research question

---

[20] Cognitive Defenses are defined, described, and handled throughout SCT literature, including in Agazarian's *System-Centered Therapy for Groups,* pp. 142-169. A list of SCT literature is at the end under "Resources."

[21] Agazarian, *System-Centered Therapy,* p. 100.

Negative Predictions [22]

A negative prediction is a scary thought about the future.

If I disagree with the Rector, the vestry won't listen to me.

If I reveal that St. Mary is someone I relate to, people will think I'm too Catholic.

I'm afraid to differ with the outspoken members at Bible study. They'll talk over me and shut me down.

Reality Test of Negative Predictions—Basic Steps [23]

1. Connect the anxiety or worry with the thought.
2. State the thought.
3. Label the thought as a negative prediction.
4. Ask about the feeling generated by the thought.
5. Make the connection between the feeling and the thought.
6. Test reality: Do you believe you can tell the future?
7. Check the belief against reality.
8. Develop curiosity about the 'here and now' experience that was defended against. [24]

Possible Responses to Step 6

The following examples illustrate how the leader can handle the variety of answers a member could make to the 6th step. The leader's remarks are italicized.

Version 1. Member believes he/she can't tell the future.

6. *Test reality: Do you believe you can tell the future?*

---

[22] Negative predictions are defined and the protocol described in *Systems-Centered Therapy for Groups*, p. 154.

[23] (Agazarian, SCT for Groups 1997), p. 154

[24] Ibid., p. 100.

"No."

7. *Since you don't believe you can tell the future, can you see that your anxiety is coming from your thought?*

8. *Are you curious about what was going on with you right before you had that thought?*

Testing Reality: Negative Prediction-Version 1	
Leader	**Lalo**
What was the thought that made you anxious?	I'm going to be an usher for the first time tomorrow. I'm afraid I'll do it wrong and look stupid.
We call that a negative prediction. What feeling is generated by that thought?	Fear. Reluctance.
Can you see that those feelings are coming from what you are thinking?	Yes.
Do you believe you can tell the future?	No.
So when you check your thought against the reality, can you see it is your thought, not the reality, that is scaring you?	Yes. I can see that.
Are you curious about what was going on with you right before you had the thought about being an usher?	Yes. [pause] I was bored. And then I felt like I shouldn't be bored.
So you had a feeling you thought you shouldn't have.	Yes.
Are you now more anxious, less anxious, or the same?	Not anxious at all. Not bored either.

Version 2. Member believes she/he can tell the future.

6. *Do you believe you can tell the future?*
   "Yes."

7. *What percent accuracy do you think you have with regard to predicting the future—10%, 50%, 70%, 90%?*
   "40%."

8. *Is anything wrong right now?*
   "No."

9. *Here is your choice: Would you rather live in the present, right now, where nothing is actually wrong? Or would you rather live in a future that has a 60% chance of not happening?*

Testing Reality: Negative Prediction-Version 2	
Leader	**Sarah**
Do you believe you can tell the future?	Yes. It's happened to me in the past.
What percent of the time are you correct—10%, 30%, 50%, 75%?	About 50%
So 50% of the time you're wrong.	Yes.
Do you want to live in the present, where nothing is wrong right now, or in a future that has a 50% chance of not coming true?	The present.
What was going on with you, right before you got anxious?	I was comparing myself to Janet. She always looks so stylish.
So you were feeling less than?	Yes.

FAQ

Q. Aren't you leaving Sarah hanging? What about her feeling that she is less than?

A. Sarah is doing work for the group, by stepping forward with an issue that is probably being held by other members as well—the issue of comparing oneself to others. Some may be feeling superior to others, while others may be aligned with Sarah. The leader's next step will be to lift up the issue and see if the group bites. For example, "Is anyone else comparing yourself to another group member?"

This kicks off the 'less than' or 'better than' subgroup. If this is a Bible study, for example, some members may be hanging back because they feel less familiar with scripture, while other members may be participating a lot because they see themselves as experts.

Making room for both subgroups to work leavens the group.

Q. So a negative prediction may illuminate an issue that is an undercurrent in the group?

A. Yes. The leader can find the theme in the negative prediction and check with the group to see if this is work for the whole group.

Q. The leader is guiding the protocol and thinking larger, right?

A. Yes. The leader is attuning both to the person and the group at the same time. The issues of individuals often echo or telegraph the group's progress up the stairs.

Q. How important is it to follow the protocol exactly?

A. Do you try to be creative with the Lord's Prayer? Certain rituals are more effective when they are followed consistently.

When you go to an official SCT training, you'll notice that the experienced leaders follow protocols precisely. The novices try to be creative with it. But being creative with a protocol puts the attention on the leader. The leader is not the focus. The focus is bringing out the defense that is slowing the group's work, whether it is a task or process group. Once those defenses are weakened, the group spurts forward.

An SCT principle that has enhanced the work of prior social scientists is that you don't have to push a group, you just have to weaken the blockades that prevent forward movement. The natural state for a group, or an individual, is to advance, so if you remove the shackles, momentum will be restored.

A windstorm on our island blew a tree across the road. Traffic stopped, until someone with a chainsaw cut through the tree. As soon as that barrier was removed, traffic resumed. A group has a similar impetus.

Q. What's with the question at the end, asking if the person is more or less anxious or the same?

A. SCT is a theory-driven/test-the-theory process. It's one of the few psychological bodies of work in which practice was/is derived first from theory. Each intervention arises from a theory; for example, the theory that anxiety is caused by a thought, in this case, about the future. After testing the reality of the negative prediction, the research question checks that theory.

Q. What if the person is still just as anxious?

A. It's likely that another cognitive defense is now in play. The leader would then ask, "Do you have another thought that is causing you to be anxious? If the member answers yes, then the leader takes her back through the appropriate procedure.

Exploring Vs. Explaining[25]

Sooner or later, probably sooner, a member will want to explain something. Why their negative prediction is logical, why they think this group is unnecessary, their reasons for being sad.

The first time this happens (after the group has begun to get

---

[25] (Agazarian, Approach 2001), p. 110.

the hang of subgrouping), the leader will have an opportunity to teach the difference between explaining and exploring.

We all tend to fall into explanations. When we explain, we are saying something we already know. It may be a story we tell over and over, familiar and comforting, even if it's a sad story.

Americans like to solve problems, so when a friend states a feeling, we are prone to explaining it. (Once you get wise to this, you'll see it everywhere.) But a feeling is not a problem and explaining keeps the conversation from leading to a discovery.

Here's an example of such a conversation.

"I was so moved by the anthem."

"Trust Tchaikovsky to get it right. That progression of minor 5ths is so effective. "

"You know a lot about music."

"Well, I did study the piccolo."

Thud.

Exploring means venturing toward the opposite direction. We open to the edge of the unknown, cross into unfamiliar territory. It is an opportunity to discover something new.

You'll hear this happen in a group when someone says, "Oh, that's a new thought!," often accompanied by a little bubble of joy.

The new discovery almost always opens a new possibility with a rush of energy and delight. Something is there that was truly not there before. We may not even have had a hint that it could be there. It's a lot more fun than the familiar.

(For those who, as children, learned that surprises are dangerous and that the unknown holds lurking beasts, it can take awhile to enjoy exploration. These members may cling longer to explaining—their port in the storm.)

A response respectful of an exploration can be a gift to both people. Here's an example:

Jody, "I was so moved by the anthem."

Rachel, "I was too. [Join] I felt my spirits lift." [Build]

Jody, "Mine did too. [Join] It was as if a door opened in my mind." [Build]

Rachel, "A door opened?" [Listening]

Jody, "I began to see my way through this situation with my sister-in-law."

Rachel, "I've got time. Do you want to explore that more?"

Jody, "If you'll explore also."

Rachel, "Of course."

Two things happened here—they made room for an exploration and they advanced their relationship. Rachel's attunement and respect, while leaving to Jody the choice about how far to explore, added a bond to their friendship. Jody signaled that it would be a two-way street, letting Rachel know she wasn't looking for a caretaker. And Rachel's join, not just active listening, signaled her interest in being a friend rather than a caretaker.

Church groups are filled with lots of generous people. When someone has a strong feeling, members may rush to help or use explaining as an attempt to help. Subgrouping gives members a way to handle this without explaining or caretaking, which can't help but lead to a one-up/one-down relationship over time. To know how to join, rather than just offer sympathy, gives members an important new tool.

When I was first learning SCT theory, I still put all my faith, as a therapist, into deep listening, that act of profound listening which helps clients find new places within themselves, places where insights bubble and shifts occur. Dr. Agazarian stated that people will work yet more deeply if they are joined.

I was skeptical and held on to my own belief for a long time. I thought if people weren't working hard and accessing pain, they wouldn't make the deeper discoveries. And then I was in SCT training groups myself and saw firsthand that people could make giant leaps forward, without suffering, as long as they were working in a subgroup, and in fact, one person didn't have to do all the work. Subgroup members, by joining and building, would circulate the issue among themselves, advancing it and advancing themselves together.

It is a process that seems deeply spiritual to me, a fulfillment of God's directive to at(tend) to each other and at the same time, a method that allows an entire group of people to become more than they knew they could be—reached only by working together.

Mind Reads[26]

A mind read is an anxiety-producing thought about what another person is thinking. We tend to not notice that this is just a thought. Many of us proceed from a mind-read into behavior that is based on the thought, without ever discovering whether or not the mind-read is a reality.

This happens willy-nilly in marriages and causes lots of unnecessary fights.

He: "You don't think I should go fishing, not when your mother is sick. You think I'm a selfish bastard. What about you? You went to that quilt show last week. And you brought home a stack of fabric. Like you need more fabric."

She: "Fish all you want. Fish all night. Smear peanut butter all over your face. Then you can just scrape it off your cheek between casting. There is no such thing as too much fabric. What about that socket set you got online? How many socket sets do you need?"

---

[26] (Agazarian, SCT for Groups 1997), p. 154.

He: "That's a European set. They are calibrated differently."

She: "Oh, so you're going to calibrate in Europe, are ya?"

I could go on, but you get it. Let's replay this conversation with reality testing.

He: "My mind read is that you don't think I should go fishing, yes or no?

She: "No."

He: "You're okay with me fishing, even though your mother is sick?"

She: "Yes. Do you believe me?"

He: "Yes!"

She: "How does it feel to find out your mind read was inaccurate?"

He: "Pretty great."

A nasty fight averted by a simple tool. (And no aspersions cast on fabric!)

Reality Testing: Mind Read[27]

The parts of a mind read reality test are:

    a. Clarify mind read

    b. Reality test

    c. Research question

Mind Read Reality Test—Basic Steps[28]

1. Connect the anxiety or worry with the thought.
2. State the thought.
3. Label the thought as a mind read.

---

[27] (Agazarian, SCT for Groups 1997), p. 100.

[28] (Agazarian, SCT for Groups 1997), p. 154

4. Ask what feeling is generated by the thought.

5. Test reality: Do you believe you can read people's minds?

6. Check the belief against reality.

7. Develop curiosity about the 'here and now' experience that was defended against.[29]

8. Ask the research question. Do you feel more anxious (worried, etc.), less anxious, or the same?

Possible responses to step 6.

One can test one's belief against reality by asking the involved person if the mind read is true. There are a variety of possible outcomes:

- The mind read is inaccurate.
- The mind read is accurate.
- The response doesn't match observed behavior, and more information is required.
- The person checking the mind read doesn't believe the other person's answer.

The following examples illustrate these variations.

Variation 1. The mind read is inaccurate.

The leader's comments are italicized.

1. *Are you thinking something that is making you anxious.*
   Lee: "Yes."

2. *What is your thought?*
   Lee: "That Jess thinks I shouldn't say anything because he has studied the Bible a lot more than I have."

3. *So your thought is one in which you are reading Jess's mind.*
   Lee: "Yes."

---

[29] Ibid., p. 100.

4. *How do you feel when you think that?*
    "Anxious, irritated. Like I should hold back."
    Do you see that your feeling comes from your own thought?
    "Yes."

5. *Do you believe you can read people's minds?*
    "Sometimes."

6. *Are you interested in finding out the reality?*
    "Yes."
    State your thought to Jess in the form of a yes or no question.
    - Lee asks, "Jess, my mind read is that you think I should keep quiet because I don't know the Bible as well as you do, yes or no?"
    - Jess: "No."

7. *How does that feel? You discovered your mind read is inaccurate.*
    Lee: "Pretty great. I'm relieved."

8. *What was going on for you, right before you noticed being anxious?*

Both feelings—anxiety and irritation—were generated by the thought. When Lee discovered the reality, the feelings dissipated.

Variation 2. The mind read is accurate.

The following examples will start with step 6.

6. *State that to Jess in the form of a yes or no question.*

    - "Jess, my mind read is that you think I should keep quiet because I don't know the Bible as well as you do, yes or no?"
    - Jess: "Yes."

This is a situation where the person taking the risk of undoing a mind read can't lose. Either the mind read is disconfirmed and they are relieved, or it is confirmed, and they feel good about perceiving the other person correctly.

Variation 3. Dissonance requiring more information.

6. *State that to Jess in the form of a yes or no question.*
    - "Jess, my mind read is that you think I should keep quiet because I don't know the Bible as well as you do, yes or no?"
    - Jess: "No."
    - Lee: "I would like more information."

Go ahead.
    - Lee asks, "When I said, 'Paul had a revolution,' you laughed. What was funny?"
    - Jess responds, "Paul had a *revelation*, on the road to Damascus."
    - Lee clarifies, "So you thought I got the word wrong?"
    - Jess laughs, "Yes, and it was funny. I pictured Paul on a bicycle, in a long robe and a beard."
    - [Group laughs, which can be a join.]
    - Lee responds, "So I wasn't thinking of that. I was thinking that when he was putting down women as a bad influence in the church, he had a revolution on his hands, because women were active followers those days, and some were leaders of the church."

Variation 4. The answer isn't believed.

6. *State that to Jess in the form of a yes or no question.*
    - "Jess, my mind read is that you think I should keep quiet because I don't know the Bible as well as you do, yes or no?"
    - Jess: "No."

7. *You look skeptical, Lee. Do you believe Jess?*
    - Lee: "No."

8. *How does it feel to not believe someone in the group?*
The beauty of this is that it doesn't have to be solved. Either

Lee is a cynical sort, reluctant to take much on face value perhaps, or Jess is reluctant to tell the whole truth. Either way, this process leaves the responsibility for each side of the issue squarely in the persons involved.

The group is a little wiser. It sees that for whatever reason— Lee being mistrustful or Jess being too nice—they don't have to do anything about it. Further observation will reveal where the chips fall. Also, both Lee and Jess, thanks to this interchange, have the opportunity to learn a lot more about themselves as the group continues. Lee may learn of a pattern of disregarding others and Jess may learn that being too nice isn't helpful.

However, the group has already been freed of any responsibility to fix either side, and it will have new energy.

The Edge of the Unknown

We underestimate the power of our fear of the unknown, even though we may organize our lives around preventing surprises. What do you do to protect yourself from the unknown?

A phrase I hear a lot in groups is, "I already knew that," or "I wasn't surprised." It's as if people don't want to be caught unaware, especially when it comes to learning about themselves.

The thrust toward explaining rather than exploring shows this. The familiar territory, the familiar story, is comforting. Any therapist or best friend who despaired when a woman stayed with an abusive man knows too well the pull of the familiar.

When a group member has relieved her anxiety based on a mind read and/or a negative prediction and is still anxious, she may well be on the edge of the unknown. The leader checks this and then, with an affirmative, goes right into the steps.

Reducing Anxiety on the Edge of the Unknown [30]

Obviously the leader is waiting for and listening to the member's answer before proceeding through the following steps.

1. *Are you anxious from being on the edge of the unknown?*
2. [Normalizing] *We are all anxious on the edge of the unknown.*
3. *What helps is to become curious. Are you curious about what you will discover if you continue to explore?*

---

[30] (Agazarian, SCT for Groups 1997), p. 90.

12 A Bell Choir Tests reality

Imagine, if you will, a church bell choir. A bell choir consists of a trained leader and a bunch of volunteers with a goal, ultimately, to promote worship. It is, therefore, a metaphor for the church-as-a-whole.

The members range in age from 12 to 92, male and female, He created them. Musical proficiency ranges from professional training to the ability to recognize four notes and count to eight.

A bell choir is not a democracy. It is governed by two entities: the composer of whatever piece is being played at the moment, and the director, a benign dictator.

A bell choir is unique in musical groups. A choir, even an orchestra, can survive the absence of some of the members. Not so with a bell choir.

Most of the ringers have two hands and, since most people can ring a bell with each hand, each person plays two of the notes of the piece. (There are times bells are changed, but we don't need to get into that.)

It's as if the keys of a piano were distributed among 12 people. If everyone presses their keys in the correct order, the tune is lovely. If two people go for coffee, the tune has holes in it.

This imaginary choir is led by a broad-minded director who sees the value of SCT skill training for the group. Together they learn functional subgrouping, and, gradually, the basic skills.

They have learned how to handle mind reads and in a post-practice session, they use their new skill:

Moze: "I'm anxious about something."

Leader: "Do you have a thought that is making you anxious?"

Moze: "Yes."

Leader: "What is the thought?"

Moze: "I think Viva is unhappy that we exchanged bells."

Leader: "So you have a mind read?"

Moze: "Yes."

Leader: "When you think that, what do you feel?"

Moze: "I feel bad, like I'm in the wrong. I want to defend myself."

Leader: "Can you see that your feeling is generated by your thought?"

Moze: "Yes."

Leader: "Do you believe you can read minds?"

Moze: "Sometimes."

Leader: "Do you want to test reality?"

Moze: "Yes."

Leader: "Put your mind read into the form of a yes or no question to Viva."

Moze: "My mind read, Viva, is that you are unhappy that Director Stave had you trade bells with me."

Viva: "Yes. It worries me that Director Stave demoted me. I liked ringing the C. C is an important bell. A and B are filler ..."

Leader: "Viva, can you hold until Moze is finished?"

Viva: "Yes."

Leader: "Moze, do you believe Viva?"

Moze: "I do."

Leader: "How does it feel to learn that your mind read is accurate?"

Moze: "A relief."

Notice that Viva also has a worry that she started to explain, but the leader kept the process clean by following through with Moze.

With Viva also presenting a worry, it's clear that the group is in the subphase of flight.

The leader can go on to help Viva test the reality behind her worry or see if there's an subgroup of people with mind reads and lead the entire subgroup through the exercise. In this case they'd use functional subgrouping to process each step of the reality test.

13 Goal Progression

As mentioned earlier, the human system—whether an individual, couple, group, or organization—has the following goal progression:

- Survival
- Development
- Transformation

When a predator is snarling in our family cave, we can't be worried about protecting the wife's flower arrangement or smashing the newly invented table. Surviving the fight is the entire goal.

Then, once the predator is the new cave floor covering, we can go back to inventing furniture. We have the space and safety then to develop.

When our survival is at risk, we can't be concerned with development. Only when survival is ensured, does development become a possibility. Thus, the first concern of an individual entering the Christian community is survival, survival of the self, the ego, one's personal perspective, one's faith and beliefs about God.

Some religions insist on a particular set of beliefs, discouraging exploration and questions. Others make room for a variety of interpretations. Members self-select their best fit, by leaving or coming back.

Within the Christian community group, as the members begin to trust the leader and the safety provided by functional subgrouping, they make the transition from surviving to developing. Each stair safely negotiated not only paves the way for development, it provides the possibility of transformation. Transformation is that exciting leap across space into newness. It brings a burst of energy from one's center that is like a firework shooting out from the heart.

The moments of transformation energize the group and they begin to glimpse a window into possibility that has never before existed for the community.

14 Stair 3—Defenses against Emotion

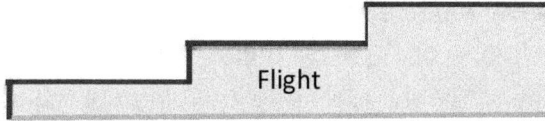

Flight

Every once in a while I take stock of my own varieties of avoidance. I have a large basket of tools for avoiding my feelings: working too hard or too long, watching TV, getting distracted by political issues, doing too much.

I'm not alone. Whether Americans are unique in over-doing nearly everything or if the entire world is avoidant, I don't know. Perhaps it is simply the human condition.

From here on, I'll use the word *experience* to refer to the actual physical sensations that let us know we are feeling something, the word *emotion* to refer to the common label, and the word *feelings* for the metaphoric description of the experience.

For example, the effervescence in my heart region is the experience, the emotional label is excitement, and the metaphoric description is that it's like a river of champagne flowing through my heart. Of course, effervescence is itself a metaphor, but the act of pausing to notice the sensation in my heart, that sensation is my experience. Labeling it joy actually takes me away from the felt experience, whereas the descriptive metaphor of champagne puts me right back into contact with my heart.

Given how easily one's primary experience can be shifted, it's surprising how many ways we avoid it. As mentioned, this first sub-phase of the authority phase is called flight. At first we are in flight through social defenses, then through cognitive defenses.

After those are weakened, we come to our defenses against emotion.

As we defuse this latter group and continue our movement toward the land beyond flight, we make way for what I think is one of the grand intentions of the Word of God.

Our physical selves are a depository of all our experiences. We can process these or suppress them. We can make room for them or sit on them. To the extent we try to ignore them, they take up residence in the body.

One of the ways we can realize this is to notice where we have tension. Tension is a muscular shield that protects us from feeling our experience. It traps and confines the physical sensations of experiences. Unfortunately, the metaphoric message, the little treasure packet riding inside an experience, is also hidden. As long as an experience is constricted, its wisdom is unavailable to us.

There are two primary ways to release tension and catch the metaphor in mid-flight. One is to deliberately go through the muscular shield and enter the cave where the experiences are stored. The other is to melt the tension through a relaxation exercise or metaphor.

Regardless of the method used, pay close attention to the first thing that happens as the tension ebbs. It might be a feeling, an image, an action by your hand or foot, an awareness, or an insight.

Whatever it is, give it voice. Speak what happens. You will, thereby, open your little treasure packet and learn something about yourself.

The leader's job is to notice when tension first presents itself in the group and lead the tense person, or subgroup, through the tension-melting process, paying particular attention to whatever shows up right after the tension is released.

Sometimes tension shows up before or at the same time as

cognitive defenses. If so, the correct order is to weaken the cognitive defenses first, then melt tension.

Notice the research question at the end. This tests the theory that released feelings relieve physical problems.

Tension Melting [31]

1. Ask person to describe the tension (tightness, bands of steel, hands around the throat),
2. And to locate the tension in the body.
3. Frame tension as a straitjacket that constricts our experience so that our awareness of our own feelings is diminished.
4. Present the choice between explaining the tension or exploring what is trapped by the tension.
5. Guide relaxation. (*A straitjacket can be relaxed. As the tension is released, notice what else happens for you. Remember to voice whatever you begin to notice.*)
6. Respond to the member's discoveries with active listening.
7. Verify usefulness of process with the research question: *Are you more tense, less tense, or the same?*

Notice that in the fourth step, the person decides whether to explore or to stop. We respect each individual's degree of willingness to learn more about themselves (thereby assigning appropriate authority).

---

[31] This is an SCT tool used to weaken somatic defenses, adapted here for use in the context of training for a Christian community. It was originated and developed by Agazarian and SCT. The original protocol, called "Undoing Tension," has additional steps. (Agazarian, SCT for Groups 1997), pp.173-176.

15 A Bell Choir Melts Tension

Tension can also pop up as unwellness. A headache, tummy ache, muscle cramp, bout of nausea, even diarrhea can signal trapped feelings.

A person expressing this can be offered the tension-melting exercise if they are curious about whether their symptoms are concealing emotions.

After rehearsal, the bell choir sat in their circle for the post-practice process session. Subgrouping proceeded efficiently, a few negative predictions handled, when Hayd leaned forward.

Hayd: "Viva, you have your hand to your forehead. Do you have a headache?"

Viva: "Yes. It's really troubling me."

Leader: "A headache can be a sign of tension. It can be a sign that your body is holding tightness against an emotion. Are you curious, Viva, as to whether this is what is happening for you?"

Viva: "Yes."

Leader: "Will you describe what you are feeling?"

Viva: "It's like I have a helmet around my head, only it's too small. It's squeezing tight. I didn't get enough sleep last night."

Leader: "Like a small helmet pressing tightly against your skull. So this could be your body constricting against a feeling, trapping feelings behind the shield around your head. You are at a fork in the road between relaxing and exploring whatever is confined by the tension, or explaining it. Which do you prefer?"

Viva: "I want to explore."

Leader: "A shield can be softened. Close your eyes, and imagine the helmet releasing and remember to notice what starts to happen as it softens. Remember to say what you notice out loud.

"So the helmet is softening and your eyes are relaxing, and your jaw is relaxing and your neck is releasing any tightness. It's like warm gel is oozing slowly down your skull taking the tension with it, slowly taking all the tightness away so that your head is completely relaxed.

Viva said, "Oh!" Her eyes popped open and she looked surprised. "I'm irritated that I hardly ever have a note in this new piece. I *hate* playing the A and B bells. I just stand there and count forever."

She looked around. "Everything is brighter. My headache is gone!"

Leader: "You discovered you've been bored and irritated that you're playing these less active bells, especially in this new piece where your part is so small.

Viva: "Yes! And I thought I should be a good sport and go along with it, because Director Stave must have a good reason, but I either want more interesting music or different bells."

Leader: "So you constricted yourself, not saying anything and going along. And now you know what you want."

Viva: "Yes! I have energy again!"

Leader: "So Viva, Hayd helped you, by noticing your gesture. Did you want to be helped?"

Viva thinks. "Yes, I can see that I wanted to be noticed. I feel so invisible with these boring bells. I'm glad Hayd noticed me."

Leader: "I'm wondering if we have an energy in the group around either wanting to be taken care of or wanting to help. Is anyone noticing this?

Hayd: "I am. I wanted to reach out to Viva and soothe her. Anyone else?"

Tension was disguising a personal issue, and then what unfolded went beyond one individual to encompass a subtle current running through the entire group. This is often an outcome of defense reduction—a discovery pertaining to the whole entity that, noticed, moves the entire community upward and onward.

In this case, the undercurrent had to do with caring and being cared about. The longing to be taken care of can be expressed by illness. In a Christian community, the urge to help is usually front and center. The minute someone shows weakness, many soldiers will line up to help.

Rather than let this be acted out, the leader has an opportunity to guide the group through the two sides of the issue. This offers the group a most important issue to subgroup—those who want to be taken care of and those who want to offer care.

The opportunity for transformation is great.

16 FORK-IN-THE-ROAD

When we're charging into patterned behavior, we may miss the road sign that shows we are at a fork-in-the-road.[32] By slowing our own process way down, we begin to notice that we have an actual choice. There *is* a road less traveled, and it goes to a better place.

My friend asked me how I was doing. I began to describe the way I had been hit by the loss of a relative. I was a few sentences in when she converted the conversation to her irritating experience on a holiday trip. (This was not a join. Interrupting with a story is different than sharing in the exploration of a common feeling.)

I felt my arousal, the desire to compete with her for mastery of the conversation, to snatch back my own air time. Before my own authority training, I'd have verbally wrestled with her, trying to get her attention back to my grief. In short order, I'm guessing, I'd have been frustrated and traveling the path through outrage, righteous indignation, and points south.

Instead, I paused. I saw the fork in the road. My first choice was between irritation and suppression of irritation. I made quick room for irritation and then another choice popped up. I now had a new fork in the road.

I could make some sort of statement about the process as I saw it, or contain my own desire to explore my grief. I chose to put my

---

[32] (Agazarian, SCT for Groups 1997) p. 303.

exploration in my sacred bowl and then could turn my attention, without any subtext of one-up or one-down, to her, fully listening and caring about her trip.

It was interesting. I actually saw her light bulb go on. She suddenly noticed herself and brought the conversation back to me with an attuned statement. And then I pulled my experience out of my bowl and had lots of room, from her, to explore it.

What a difference—to actually see that I had a choice, to have methods I could use to be okay within myself while she did what she needed to do. Stepping back like this, we can see how this is a part of the phase of learning to give and take appropriate authority. We can also see, from a spiritual perspective, the grace in the way that conversation evolved.

Whenever we encounter a defense—an opportunity to avoid a feeling—we are at a fork in the road. By slowing down, we can see where each path will lead and make a deliberate decision about the type of experience we would like to have.

The leader can lift this up using language appropriate to the group's skills and level of training so that members can perceive the fork-in-the-road and make a conscious choice. Examples:

- *Have you noticed you are at a fork in the road between feeling anxious or testing reality? Which path do you want to take?*
- *You are at a fork in the road. One path leads to the part of yourself that was unavailable to you, the other path defends against that experience. Which path do you want to take?*
- *Boredom has entered the group. That could mean you are at the fork in the road between an awareness that aggressive energy is starting to flare versus constricting against that energy.*

17 CONTAINERS

If we don't suppress, squash, avoid, act out, or drink to handle feelings, what can we do? Make room for them. Making room for a feeling causes a lot less trouble for everyone.

The various defenses cause way more trouble than the experience defended against. And that is what we are missing when we are defended—an experience. An experience that carries wisdom (and something else even more valuable).

Embedded in the previous chapters are some of the answers. Methods for making room for one's feelings and experiences include:

- Active listening
- Joining
- Containing

By contain, I don't mean putting feelings in a box and shutting the lid, but providing a container, a bowl, to hold them.

Notice the first two methods involve at least one other person. This is, I think, an example of the Word of God made manifest. We humans are constructed so as to require another person when things get hard. When we don't or can't turn to another person, that's when we grab a defense.

We are trained early in life to either make room for feelings or to hide from them. Children who are listened to, comforted, shown how to use their bodies as an open container, grow up knowing how to allow themselves to experience. Children who are shushed, punished, ignored, given candy, or made to work or take care of others learn to hide from pain.

Undoing this training takes lots of time and lots of successful healthy alternative experiences. It requires a decision: I will make room for my own life's experiences. It also requires a method.

The methods described in this book and the far more detailed and comprehensive methods taught at an SCT conference provide an increasing capacity to differentiate among experiences that have been lumped together in a big overwhelming pile.

Learning to trace the difference between frustration and irritability and the impulses that arise from it, or pausing long enough to see that you are at a fork in the road between acting against yourself versus making room for a feeling (and the energy and wisdom accompanying it) are skills that bring back to you pieces of yourself that have been split off and tucked away.

We can have such an automatic response of shoving an intense experience into muscle fibers that we aren't just tightened against the experience, we aren't just tense, we've also lost all awareness that a primary experience was even there in the first place. This means we've split off a part of ourselves and hidden it from our own eyes. It's like a box placed so quickly into the attic that we've forgotten there ever was a box or what was in it.

Each of these techniques resurrects a split part of yourself and the joy in this recovery of self is what sends people away from their training group with renewed energy and a new sense of wholeness. They have actually re-found themselves.

Metaphors

Jesus often used parables to teach. The metaphors he used imparted a universal reality. Using metaphor to experience or to relate experiences can offer a greater reality than an ordinary technical explanation.

Sports reporting is full of metaphors—he blasted through the defense, the skater soared like a feathered swan.

Contrast that with the literal explanation—the running back put his head down and shoved it into the chests of three giant strong men, pushing and pushing until they fell down and he gained yardage past them. The skater dug the tip of her blade into the ice, thrusting herself into the air where she traveled 6 feet before landing, each skate regaining purchase smoothly.

Which version gave you the whole picture?

Sacred Bowl Exercise

If we have not been taught how to create a container within ourselves for our experiences, we are more vulnerable to requiring a defense to handle them. With this exercise, we use a metaphor to help ourselves experience. It is a tool we can use over and over.

This exercise is more effective when it takes place after centering, after undoing distractions, and after the group knows how to subgroup and explore. It is also better if cognitive defenses have been through reality testing.

The leader guides this exercise. Pause after each instruction.

1. With feet flat on the floor, hands relaxed, spine in alignment, begin to center.
2. Let your breath slow and deepen.
3. Follow your breath into your inner spaces.
4. Notice the space you make when you breathe in.
5. How big is that space? How much room do you make?
6. Notice, what is in that space?
7. Notice, how are you reacting to what is in that space? Are you drawn to it, or are you tightening against it? Are you trying to duck away from it?
8. Decide: Do you want to fend it off or do you want to

practice a skill?

9. See if you can turn on your curiosity. Can you become curious enough to explore the experience?

10. If so, imagine that a large bowl is inside your center.

11. Allow the bowl to hold your experience or feeling.

12. The bowl can expand and be as large as it needs to be in order to contain the experience.

13. Make plenty of space inside yourself for the experience. And the bowl.

14. Notice what it is like to make room for the experience.

15. Notice what the experience does. What happens to it?

16. *What metaphor describes the feeling? You can say it out loud.* [Expressing the metaphor softly out loud is akin to praying out loud for the sick in the prayers for the people—a common expression that does not have to be responded to.]

17. Continue to watch the experience. Continue to find metaphors to describe it.

18. In a moment, I'll ask you to turn to another person and say the metaphor. You can each go back and forth expressing your own metaphor. The act of sharing your metaphors is the join. Keep your focus on yourself and your own metaphors.

19. When you are ready, open your eyes and share your metaphors.

The leader waits while the metaphor sharing has energy. When it begins to subside, the leader then directs members to begin functional subgrouping of their experience. The two subgroups are likely to be some variation of those for whom the exercise worked and those who felt blocked.

The group is strengthened by this skill for it gives members a language for encouraging each other to contain, rather than throw off or defend against feeling.

A member of one of my training groups would spread his hands apart while supporting someone in containing a difficult feeling. It was a visual metaphor for making room and one that I picture for myself when internal room is needed.

Skill Training Increases Options

After this exercise is taught as a part of group training, persons can also use it on their own. Remembering that the first phase of system, group, and human development is the authority phase, we can claim authority over our own choice to experience or not experience when we have a method that allows us to do so.

One beauty of SCT processes is that the individual and group are given the skills to make a different choice before they are presented with that choice.

When they learn to subgroup, they are given the experience of being joined, before they have to choose whether or not to feel. A join is an opening experience. We are opened to more inside ourselves. And if we choose to risk again, we are again joined, and we open to more.

This is the importance of the leader ensuring joins above all else. When members can trust they'll never work alone, they have amazing safety for exploration into the unknown.

And where does the unknown exist?

Inside ourselves? Outside ourselves? In our own reactions to all that happens?

18 Transition From Person to Member

The beginning stair-steps help everyone cross the boundary from their individual person systems so that they can take up their roles as members of this particular group which is meeting in this actual moment.

For example, the experience one has in "one's personal context (where the goal is personal growth) is different from one's member role in the subgroup system (where the goal is to resonate with others) or in the context of the group-as-a-whole system (where the goal is to develop an environment that will potentiate...goals)."[33]

Gaining consciousness of context is an awareness that can benefit church members in all their worlds, not just the one within your sanctuary.

Person System

You are a system. You have the self you present to others and your inner self. You carry a set of complex feelings. You have physical structures that hold other physical structures or that allow the physical plant of your body to operate 24/7.

Your thoughts and feelings have a lot of power over your physical body and your physical body knows things that your conscious mind doesn't.

---

[33] (Agazarian and Gantt, Autobiography 2000), p. 240.

When you are ensconced in your person system, you are viewing the world as an individual. You are reacting to others from a personal perspective.

Effective relationships require that you bring your personal energy and awareness across the boundary to enter your role as a member of the relationship.

Member Role

When you enter a relationship system the group will be more effective if you take up your role as a member of that group. Operating from your functional member role is different from operating from your person role.

In the member role, you view things differently. You take on the perspective of a member. You become able to discriminate when your impulses arise from your person system and you gain discipline in acting concordant with the member role, either tabling the content of a person system impulse until later, or channeling that energy and information in a way that is appropriate to the work of the group.

Examples of inappropriate intrusion of the person system into member roles include being late, texting during a meeting, using non-resonant humor or excessive jargon or some other attention-drawing device to manipulate the group's response or treatment.

Leader Role

The leader role consists of setting and keeping boundaries, promoting discriminations, tracking the progress of the group through the phases of development, intervening appropriately to teach the group new skills, and vectoring the group toward positive goals. It's a complicated role involving constant multi-tasking.

The leader must be especially careful to watch for the intrusion of her own person system needs into her leadership function.

An example of this is when, years ago, I used chatter to elicit group sympathy when I didn't know how to operate a machine.

As the leader, I should have either familiarized myself with the machine beforehand or designated someone as the assistant in charge of media. I was using the machine to discharge my nervousness. I was looking to the group for succor.

This insertion of person into a leader function is distracting, irritating, and sets a tone of muddy boundaries, all negative influences on the progress of a group.

Making Distinctions

A similar manipulation can happen when individuals stay in their person system after the group starts working. Someone presenting themselves as cute or needy or smarter or controlling is someone who isn't managing their personal needs or energy, who isn't taking up the responsible role of membership.

Groups are smart and they pick up on this sort of appeal or manipulation. It tells them they are not entirely safe, because they can't count on everyone knowing appropriate boundaries. They will automatically limit their degree of risk.

Church groups, believing that they should be loving and caring if at all possible, tend to reward person behavior in group settings by rushing in with caretaking (including letting someone who needs to be seen as smarter go unchallenged when he is wrong). Do they resent it? It would be human to do so, and this resentment at being used can sink into that crowded basement holding other rejected feelings.

Long, long ago, while the smoke was still rising from Sherman's fires, I led a workshop in my church in Atlanta. A person in the group stayed in his person system role, arriving drunk, never having read the materials, never prepared. A lot of group time was spent either protecting the other members, explaining things to him, or trying to stick to the agenda despite his inappropriate interruptions.

Finally I quietly, between sessions, removed him from group. Most of the group were outraged with me. They were willing to forego the discoveries potent in the class to do their Christian duty by accepting a fractious member with no capability for attunement and no ability to take up group membership.

And outrage, as we'll see soon, is a way to avoid anger. Outrage toward me was more acceptable to them than anger at someone they saw as needy.

When a group is first learning the skills presented here, they may not know that there is a difference between person and member behavior, which is why a leader who has experienced this distinction is preferred. The leader will gently teach them while guiding them into effective membership.

Contexts

As a member, you will be nested in the system of the subgroup, which is nested in the group-as-a-whole. When you take up your membership, your member skills advance both the subgroup and the group-as-a-whole. You become capable of making the distinction between looking at yourself and others from a person perspective versus seeing yourself and others from a member perspective.

An example of a way you automatically do this is when you go to work. When you go through the doors of your workplace, you enter your member role in that environment. You view things from the perspective of employee, manager, teacher, trainer, worker, or supervisor.

You wouldn't be successful if you stayed only in your person system at work—if you talked to customers about your problems or asked a staff member to balance your personal checkbook or ran to your boss every time you had a mood change. You know instinctively that such actions would not be appropriate. It would not be member behavior.

(And when you see someone inserting their personal needs at work, it stands out. They lose respect fast.)

One of the ways married people get into trouble is by approaching a member issue solely from their person systems.

Mutt: "I hate that you throw your keys on the tray beside the door."

Jeff: "Who made you president? I like having my keys next to the door."

Mutt: "It's untidy. You should hang your keys from a hook like I do, then the surface would be uncluttered."

Jeff: "Where would I put the remote? It sits right next to my keys. In the tray. With my chapstick. And my change. Maybe you should use that Asian money that has a hole in it, then you could hang up your money."

Mutt: "Why don't you just sit on your tray if you like it so much?"

You can probably tell this showed up as part of the authority phase. Let's see if member behavior makes a difference.

Mutt: "I have irritation about where we put our keys, anybody else?"

Jeff: "I join you. I'm irritated too. I'd like to center, anybody else?"

Mutt: "Okay."

They go to the living room and center themselves.

Jeff: "I like putting my keys, phone, and change near the door. I care about having all my things together so that I don't have to look for each thing. I hate having to search for my keys when I leave, anybody else?"

Mutt: "I join you on not liking to search for my stuff. And I care about surfaces being uncluttered. Seeing that pile of stuff is irritating. That's why I like to hang everything from the hook by the door to the garage. It's out of the foyer and the place is tidy. Anybody else?"

Jeff: "I like tidiness too. But not all of my things can be hung up. And I use the front door since I take the bus to work, so when I come in, I like to just drop it all at once, there. I don't want to have to put each thing away. Anybody else?"

Mutt: "I can join on not wanting to put each single item away, especially when you have to use it all the next day. What if we got a different container, a bowl, a decorative one, with a lid? You could put the bowl on the bookshelf, drop all your stuff in, and then put the lid on it? Anybody else?"

Jeff: "I love that idea. And I love to shop. I've wanted to check out that new shop on Front Street."

Mutt: "Me too. Let's go."

Subgrouping saved the day, and provided the simple solution. In the first round, Mutt and Jeff were both quickly defended. When we're defended, we don't have access to our creativity. In fact, we become more and more closed off to the creative compromise. By centering and subgrouping, they helped themselves cross the boundary into their member roles.

It takes practice to tell the difference between your member role and your person system when you are at church, because a spiritual life is intensely personal. For now, just having these definitions in mind will help you start to see differently. Most people try this on, don't really get it, and then one day, the insight just pops into their awareness. So don't be concerned if this isn't registering.

Crossing the Boundary

We've already been practicing skills which help individuals cross the boundary into their member role. Centering, undoing distractions, undoing cognitive defenses all help people take up their membership in the group.

Being a member does not mean letting go of personal concerns, it means seeing how to use your energy and intelligence to advance

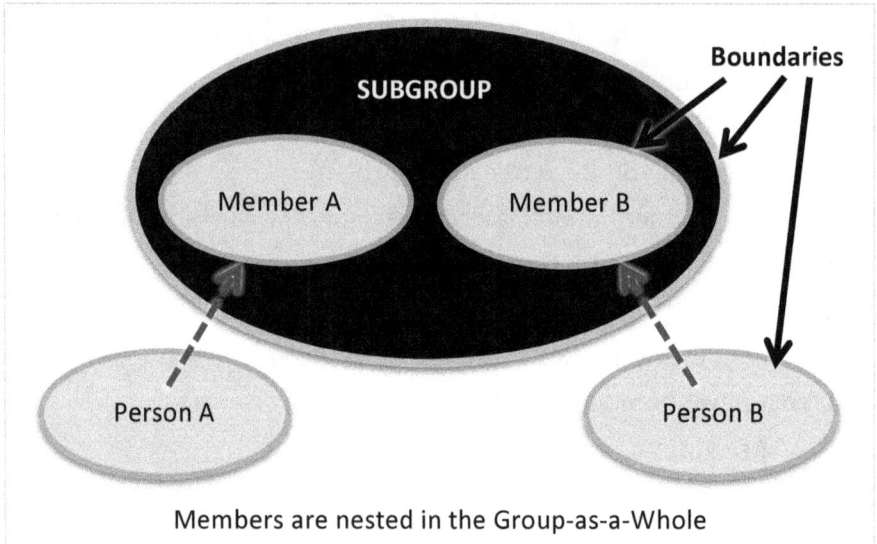

Members are nested in the Group-as-a-Whole

the group. It means paying attention to what is going on inside you while paying attention to what is happening in the group and what stage the group is in.

Membership is advanced citizenship.

In the member role, we use these skills:

- Attunement
- Resonance
- Respect of structural boundaries
- Discipline

Attunement means paying attention to what's going on with a subgroup or another member when you have personal energy to bring into the group. When a subgroup is in a deep exploration, it means waiting to bring in your difference—your different energy or different exploration—until they've gotten to their discovery.

Resonance means joining another person at their same level of energy or involvement. If someone is weeping as they describe a moving experience, joining with a giggle would not be resonant. We are challenged to access a similar level of experience when we join with our similarity.

Respect of Structural Boundaries. As members, we are in our seats ready to work, all personal needs taken care of, before crossing the time boundary at the start of group.

Discipline. If we find ourselves in opposition to an idea, as members, we say, "I have a difference." (We don't wait till break and gossip in a corner about our difference regarding someone else's idea.)

If someone shares and hasn't been joined, we look inside ourselves to find some sort of an honest join so that no soldier is left behind.

Wearing your name tag is member behavior. In every group, there are those who resist wearing name tags. This is an example of the authority phase made manifest—that pull between joining versus making a statement about being separate or individual. This is a great topic to subgroup to bring the issue to the fore.

Being late is almost always an authority issue in action. I used to be late often and actually had a sort of pleasure in the resistance of it, until I had to face the fact that this was my way of clinging to my own authority. I was opposing submission to authority by following my own time frame. Of course, now and then, we are unavoidably detained, but I now hate being late for I understand it is not member behavior.

Baptism is a powerful example of making the transition from person to member. Jesus, by submitting himself to John's baptism, demonstrated to all onlookers the process for crossing the threshold into the fellowship of believers in the new message about God. Jesus embodied the most powerful human authority on earth, yet he humbled himself and became a member.

Even if we were baptized as infants, by renewing our baptismal vows, we are taking up our membership as Christians.

Here's How

If I get excited about something that is happening in group, that excitement is in my person system. Then when I say, "I'm excited by Al's suggestion and I want to explore that possibility, anybody else?" I'm bringing my excitement into the group through member behavior. Holding my energy under my hat is person system. Bringing my energy appropriately into group is member behavior.

What if I feel shy? That is in my person system. But when I say, "I'm feeling shy and I'm wanting to hold back, anybody else?" I'm starting a subgroup and that is taking up the member role.

A bit earlier in the chapter I mentioned people being cute or controlling, needy, or feeling smarter. When we act these things out, trying to get noticed or taken care of, we're operating from our person systems, but when we bring these impulses into the group for exploration, we are being effective members.

Examples:
- "I'm noticing the impulse to be seen as cute, anybody else?"
- "I'm wanting to control what's going on here, anybody else?"
- "I'm feeling really needy, anybody else?"
- "I'm wanting to be taken care of, anybody else?"

The explorations thus started can lead to marvelous discoveries, not just by the members about themselves, but also about the group as a whole. Each situation is probably being sparked by some undercurrent in the group, which can only be discovered by exploring the deep experiences that people often conceal, not just from others, but themselves as well. The group, then, becomes wiser and more self aware.

Another skill is also thereby fostered—self observation. Gaining the capacity to catch yourself in the act of wanting attention or wanting to hide, and revealing this rather than acting it out, assists other members in noticing their own impulses.

Members become better self observers.

Your person system knows your style, your preferences, your reactions. Member behavior means bringing that information into the group in a way that the group can do something with it. If irritation, for example, is acted out, everyone's defenses go up. People retreat to their person systems and there is too much space among individuals. If irritation is, instead, stated with an invitation to join, the act of finding a similarity and the intention of using it as work brings energies together to find the path through.

These disciplines are member behavior. They change the group dynamic in a marvelous way.

Part 2: Advanced Skills

A church is closer to a family than a business. It's a situation where we want to feel that our entire selves are welcome, and where we hope to process our flaws.

Even though churches may make a point of inviting the attendance of sinners, the degree to which we can reveal or must hide our sins depends on the type of sin and the safety and openness of the congregation.

Much sinfulness is a result of two factors: the mishandling of anger and adaptations we've made to survive. Either of these can be taken too far, of course, past the province of the laity of the church and into the hands of the justice system.

But ordinary garden variety flaws arising from these factors can be much improved by a daring skill set. In the following chapters, these skills will be offered.

The next stair-steps address internal processes that are largely unconscious. They offer ways to bring hidden messages and internal rabble-rousers into awareness.

Do unconscious processes affect our church groups? Certainly. If we can surface these safely, is it life-giving? For heaven's sake, yes.

Is this therapy? Is a transition from hidden to known just the province of therapist offices, or can it also be a spiritual process and within the purview of the church?

We are inviting, through the practice of these more advanced skills, a look into our deeper selves. How can we tell if we've crossed the line from spiritual skillfulness into a therapeutic situation?

The model that may have help for us is found in recovery circles. At a 12-step meeting, such as AA or any other anonymous program, the leaders are from the group, usually not trained in a counseling profession. Yet, members share raw, piercing mistakes safely, accessing deep anguish and powerful regret.

They are held in safety by traditions such as anonymity, strictures against gossiping, and by treating each person's words as entirely about that person and no one else. Members hold a high degree of resonance. If one person goes to a profound place, no one unthinkingly makes a distracting jest. These traditions and the unabashed acceptance in AA of each person as a sinner gives each person safety.

I invite you to create traditions for your own church community. Use functional subgrouping to design a list of behaviors you will all willingly commit to follow. Some items for consideration:

- Anonymity
- Confidentiality
- Gossip/Triangulation

Clearly, if someone falls apart and can't put themselves back together, the next stop is a therapist's office. But that extreme is unlikely if the entire group is using functional subgrouping. Then, every member is advancing into deeper territory together. The risk is shared. The risk level is defined. The support of the subgroup is trusted. The members have learned by now that they will never work alone.

Thus, the greatest security in the following chapters comes from skilled, experienced subgrouping. It keeps the work of the group as a common exploration.

19 STAIR 4—DEFENSE AGAINST FRUSTRATION

We have earned our way to the money seats.

Every time we weaken a defense, we nudge a door to a part of ourselves we've walled off. And until we practice these skills regularly, we won't even know we have keys to spare rooms holding treasures. Only when a piece of ourselves reconnects, only then do we suddenly notice a greater sense of wholeness and a spurt of energy.

It's like an internal antiques roadshow. This piece is discovered, then that piece, bits of variable antiquity. This is worth its face value, that, a bit more, but, oh, that, that is priceless!

The priceless part is just ahead, the part of ourselves that has been at the bottom of the back closet in the far corner of the basement, inaccessible due to our defenses against frustration.

As with the previous pairings—anxiety as a defense against thoughts, tension as a defense against emotion—we are dealing here with a primary feeling and a secondary feeling. The primary feeling is some aspect of frustration, the secondary feeling is the pain or arousal that is a result of constricting against the primary feeling.

Each exploration helps dissipate the secondary feeling so that the origin, the primary experience, can be discovered and transformed.

We protect ourselves from the experience of frustration through a series of defenses that start with outrage and, after some intermediary events, culminate at hatred. By the time we, in this book, get to hatred, we'll be beyond the scope of what a non-SCT trained leader should try to handle but we'll talk about that when we get there. (And yes, hatred is a defense and a subphase of the authority phase, close to the brink that tumbles into intimacy.)

(By the way, if you've skipped to this stair-step without learning and practicing the tools of the previous steps, you'll be venturing into this challenge without your complete toolkit. It's your choice, of course, but if this doesn't work out, go back and take the stair-steps in order. Being fortified for this next segment makes it work out in a more complete way.)

The secret to handling the various intensities of anger is to increase our capacity for containment, which the previous steps taught. Containing as in holding, the way a fireplace holds a fire, so that the heat and energy are available without singeing anything, gives us the confidence to allow ourselves acquaintance with our own heat and fiery energy.

Until now, the defenses that arrived on each stair were in the service of flight, flight from joining, flight from conflict, flight from sensation. Each of the interventions moved the person and the group up the staircase through the flight subphase of the authority phase.

The next subphase is a transition from the flight subphase to the fight subphase.[34]

We bring to this subphase a complex mixture of skills, experiences, and beliefs. We may have been taught healthy ways of handling anger; we may have observed respectful, effective expressions of anger. Most of us, however, have tiny little anger

---

[34] (Agazarian and Gantt, Autobiography 2000), pp. 208-209.

toolkits, consisting of fire extinguishers and suppressants.

We also may be laden with heavy beliefs about how good Christians are supposed to handle anger—by turning cheeks or "turnething" away wrath with a soft answer—occasional righteous anger allowed for moneylenders in the Temple.

For a society that had no trouble trading in donkeys for SUVs and stone tablets for ipads, we sure cling to the old rulebook when it comes to anger.

As anger starts to be felt in a group, its progress—and unity—may come to a screeching halt if the group isn't helped. The group will split. Some members will act anger out. Others will act it in. Not surprisingly, Dr. Agazarian has a tool for each situation.

(By the way, remember that a true SCT training group, where the entire focus is skill learning, has a leader that is trained to titrate the group's exposure to issues and break steps down into tiny toe prints. All SCT students are marinated in theory. Therefore, I recommend that anyone planning to take up a leader function using this book, also read one of the books listed in the appendix in order to get the theoretical underpinning that holds the techniques together.)

To Frustrate

The Latin origins of the word, *frustrate*, are interesting. A commonly agreed on original meaning is *to disappoint*, derived from *in vain*. In vain—yes! What a perfectly spot-on meaning for *frustrate*.

Other original meanings included to:

- Deceive
- Trick
- Elude
- Reject

- Cheat

Clearly, whichever definition fits our experience, frustration is a deep and complex experience against which we erect bulwarks.

Acting Outward Defenses against Frustration

Acting out has a bad rap and deservedly so, for lots of reasons. It is hurtful to others, it tears the fabric of a relationship, and it hurts us too. The hurt to ourselves is at least threefold.

- Sooner or later, acting out puts more space in a relationship than we probably want.
- Acting out keeps us from discovering the treasure hidden in the corner of the closet at the back of the basement.
- Acting out doesn't satisfy internal ire for very long.
- Acting out can become addictive.

Gossip is an example.

Question: What is gossip?

Answer: Verbal discharge of anger by targeting a difference.

Many years ago, I was at an office party in the old south. Staff members consisted of both dark and light-skinned races. The group was jovial, easily social, as southerners are. A point came where the only people left at the party were the light-skinned folk. And then came the racist, gossipy comments. I was truly shocked. Partly, because this was a philanthropic organization with a lot of integrated outreach. Partly because I had believed that this staff was higher minded, way beyond the racism of the past.

So, what was going on? The group was targeting a difference. It was discharging anger.

Did the target deserve the anger? No. Scapegoating is about finding a place to dump feelings we don't want to own. We convince ourselves that the target deserves this fire because of some way they are too different, but what's really going on is that we are trying to get frustration out of our own bodies.

Since we are not connecting our frustration to the true cause, it won't be satisfied. That group did not walk away cleansed. They would soon find other targets for their lava.

Their relationships would fragment. Everyone there had to know that they weren't safe from any of the others. A group that is looking for a target will, sooner or later, target each other. Any difference could come under fire.

The group was acting outward. Acting outward is one of the two possible directions we can go if we want to defend against frustration.

Examples of verbally acting outward in a hostile fashion include blaming, complaining, righteous indignation, sarcasm, and (the subtle one) negative implying. The more of a case we can make for the unsuitability of the difference we are targeting, the more justified and rational we appear to ourselves.

At one point in my training, I was expounding on the faults of our trainer. My classmates tried to vector me in a more productive direction, but I wasn't having any of it. I was building a case on blocks of rational examples. They barely hid their smiles because they knew I was in a fit of outrage and righteous indignation. They knew I was not containing my own angry energy and they had the capacity to observe without either criticizing me or getting triggered themselves—a stellar example of operating from personal authority.

The irony is, that in that particular training module, I kept blanking out on the outrage lesson. I kept not remembering the protocol for undoing outrage, kept forgetting it was a part of the defense hierarchy.

You can learn from my denial. If, here, in this book, there's a section that keeps slipping away from you, a stair-step you keep forgetting, you could well be in that defense at the moment. If so, you can either back down a step and fortify your foundation, or take a closer look at yourself, your behavior, and your thoughts, and see if you can detect what is hiding inside you.

Outrage

Why do you make me look at injustice? Why do you tolerate wrong?
Destruction and violence are before me; there is strife, and conflict abounds.

Habbakuk gives us a good example of outrage (1:3). In fact, for an excellent tour of the continuum of angry expression, read the book (in the *Bible*) of *Habbakuk*. (Notice that God never gets angry with Habbakuk for being angry with Him.)

Outrage is our entry into the defenses against the exploration of frustration. It's one of my favorites. Our world offers endless scope for outrage. Throw me almost any topic and I can find a fitting outrage:

- Cars—Tailgaters, emission standards, drunk drivers, texting while driving—don't.
- Birds—Kidnapping rainforest tropicals for pets, misleading hummingbirds into hanging around by feeding them past midsummer so they don't migrate and then starve in winter.
- Worms—OK, I'm stumped. I can't find an outrage for worms. But the day is young.

Here's a shocking idea. Outrage is not a feeling. It's a thought. It's a thought about the thing that is frustrating you. Same with sarcasm and righteous indignation—these are all thoughts about a person or situation, even if they sound really angry.

Unpacking Outrage[35]

When outrage surfaces, it is an opportunity for the group to pause at the fork in the road between targeting others versus exploring frustration.

We unpack outrage by following steps similar to the tools used to weaken cognitive defenses.[36]

- Notice what you are doing.
- Notice that thoughts are driving your behavior.
- Notice that these thoughts are actually a distraction from your actual experience.
- Choose whether or not you will make room for your experience.

Sometimes, our thoughts include a belief that we understand a universal principle that we think everyone should know and abide by. Bringing out this belief is useful, as it uncovers a way we think we are more correct or righteous.

Furthermore, we enjoy being more right or aware or skilled or ethical than the other guy. Who wouldn't? Outrage can be quite pleasurable. When we really look at ourselves as we frolic inside the bubble of outrage, we may realize it is enjoyable.

We're allowed to enjoy that pleasure on our way to deeper self-discovery. In fact, I find that acknowledging the pleasure is relaxing, which creates an opening for the experience that was being defended against through outrage.

The following is an example of how the leader might guide the

---

[35] The tool used in SCT groups is called "Undoing Outrage," originated by Agazarian and developed in SCT. Discussion of the cognitive nature of outrage and the pleasure derived from it is in *Systems-Centered Therapy for Groups,* p. 213.

[36] (Agazarian, SCT for Groups 1997), pp. 213-214.

process:

1. *Are you noticing that you are expressing outrage?*
2. *What thoughts are driving your communication?*
3. *You seem to be saying you are more* _____ *than the other person/group. How does that feel?*
4. *Are you curious about what feelings inside you are being concealed by these outward-facing thoughts?*
5. *If you pause to look inside yourself, what do you discover?*

[Based on what the person reveals, guide him/her in making room for the feeling and adding an *anybody else* so that it becomes the work of the group.]

Exploring Outrage	
Leader	**Member**
	I'm walking on the trail at the park, quiet, beautiful, mist curling around the spruces. And I start hearing chatter, chatter, chatter. I come around a curve and there's a woman on a cell phone, talking away. No awareness of where she is or how intrusive...
Are you noticing you are expressing outrage?	Yes.
Are you interested in exploring it?	Yes.
What thoughts are sparking your outrage?	A state park forest is a sanctuary. It ought to be respected as such. There ought to be places where a person is safe from cell phones. People who use cell phones any time and place are rude.

You seem to be saying you are more ____ than that woman was. Fill in the blank.	I'm more aware. I'm more respectful. I'm more tuned in.
What's it like to feel more enlightened?	Feels good.
Can you let yourself feel the pleasure in that?	Feeling it.
Are you curious what feelings inside you are being concealed by these outward-facing thoughts?	Yes.
If you pause and look inside, what do you discover?	I am full of fire. I am so angry that my serenity was interrupted. The fire is raging inside me, I want to burn that woman's cell phone. I want to take all the phones and turn them to ashes.
The way your peaceful morning was turned to ashes?	Yes. Yes!

20 More Stair 4—Acting In

If we don't act outward, in order to avoid frustration, our other direction is to act in. When we act in, we turn our anger against ourselves. We target ourselves. The immediate result is a loss of energy. As we get good at exploring acting in, we can notice the loss of energy that is a gray flag signaling the onset of depression.

We know well, by now, that depression can have a chemical basis that is righted by the appropriate medication. Depression can also be caused by targeting ourselves and this can augment clinical depression.

Even if we have no chemical imbalance, we can sink as a result of acting in. Self-criticism, self-castigation, driving ourselves relentlessly, impossibly high standards, passivity, helplessness, are all ways we can target ourselves.

The whoosh of air leaving the group, the group going dead in the water, signals the appearance of denied aggression. If a leader tries to push the group at this point, without helping them identify the root, the aggression may well be turned against the leader, if not actively within the group session, later, in the restroom or in the car on the way home. Thus the depressed energy will then be reversed into acting outward. Either way, an opportunity is missed.

By identifying what is in the group and giving the group the option of exploring it, personal and group authority is advanced.

Leader: *"The group has suddenly lost energy. I wonder if some members have begun to feel frustrated or aggressive and are trying to clamp that down. You might be at the fork in the road between exploring frustration and defending against it. Is there a subgroup that is ready to explore the defense of constricting against aggression or frustration?"*

Exploring Depressive Acting In [37]

1. *Pause to notice the non-experience of depression, to notice that flatness, that loss of energy.*
2. *Think back to the last time [in this group] you had energy.*
3. *Move forward in time just a little bit to the point you lost your energy.*
4. *Now back up, just a bit. What happened between the time you had energy and the point where you lost it?*
5. *Something happened. It might have been a feeling inside you or a thought.*

At this point, the leader pays close attention to the slightest clue offered by the member. The member is bringing something up that was truly unconscious and they may only be able to grasp a fragment. That fragment may not make sense to the member and they may try to dismiss it. Trust that the fragment is pulling the whole piece behind it and it matters. The leader can use active listening and an encouragement to relax the diaphragm to make room for the understanding that is trying to emerge.

6. *[If the member can't pull it out, the leader relaxes and normalizes this.] So something is trying to emerge, and it may*

---

[37] Agazarian has identified depression as aggression turned inward. The above questions are an example of bracketing, her technique to facilitate discovery of a stifled impulse. For a fuller understanding of theory and practice, look at *Systems-Centered Therapy for Groups*, Chapter 8, specifically, pp. 199-203.

need time. Can you make room for waiting to learn more?

7. [The group has been working along, and someone else may well be noticing the emergence of a similar experience.] *Is anyone else aware of an emerging thought or feeling?*

Exploring Acting Inward	
Leader	**Member**
Is anyone else aware of losing energy?	I am.
Do you want to explore it?	Yes.
Can you think back to the last time you had energy?	It was while our subgroup was working.
So you had energy while you were exploring the parking lot issue?	Yes.
And then what happened?	The other subgroup started working.
So you lost energy when the other subgroup started working?	Yes. Oh, actually, it was when you asked if we were ready for the other subgroup to work.
Ah, when I asked that, you lost energy?	Yes.
Did you have a thought at that moment?	Yes. I didn't want to stop working. I thought we were getting somewhere.
Did something keep you from saying that thought?	I thought you were the leader of the group and we ought to go along with what you said.
So you had a thought that you kept silent. Did you have a feeling about being interrupted?	[Pause] I was angry about being interrupted. I felt stopped.
Can you make room for that feeling now?	[Pause] I'm angry that you interrupted us.
Do you want to be joined?	Yes. Anybody else?

This is a moment of great possibility for the group, and in a Christian community, a fragile one. To the ordinary fears of aggression that many of us have, we are carrying 3000 or more

years of admonishment to
suppress anger.

Backing away at this
point leads right to the

> A patient man has great
> understanding, but a quick-tempered
> man displays folly. [Proverbs 14:29]

Achilles' heel of the Christian community, diverting frustration
toward an acceptable target. If the group gets afraid or if a leader in
the church gets triggered into trying to control the group through
Bible verses or castigation, the constriction will return.

Fear in the group is easily handled. Simply back down the
stairs and fortify the foundation by using the tool for weakening
anxiety. A negative prediction or mind read about anger is scaring
the group.

If a leader in the church makes some sort of pronouncement
against the group or the group process, vector that toward subgroup
work. "Hal is presenting an exploration for a subgroup." Possible
frames for the church leader's comments could be:

This is very hard work. How does it feel to tackle something so hard?

So-and-so proposes that we are acting against the teachings of the Bible.
*Would you be interested in exploring each side of this issue? Can we find two
subgroups here?*

Possible subgroups:

- Is there a difference between the letter of the *Bible* and the
  spirit of the *Bible*?
- Feeling the need to be controlled (for example, by the
  Bible) versus not wanting to be controlled.

Question: What is the undercurrent that is so frightening to the
group at this level of work?

Answer: It is on the brink of discovering a big no-no in the
Christian world.

21 STAIR 5—DEFENSE AGAINST RETALIATION

The lovely thing about a designated church authority standing up and casting a judgment over the group is that he is enacting right in front of everyone a Christian's greatest denial.

We really, really don't want to notice that we want to hurt someone back.

You kick me. I want to kick you back. The desire to get even is as old as Cain and Abel. That's pretty old. And throughout the *Bible* we see object lessons in the folly of retaliation. God is not happy with it.

Turning the other cheek—that's our model.

However, God didn't say we weren't supposed to notice how we felt. We just aren't supposed to act on it.

> In your anger do not sin.
> [Ephesians 4:26]

That critical difference leads to the grace of this training for a church community. Because if the members don't have a way of exploring the impulse to retaliate it will get acted on—either acted out or acted in. Acting out causes a community mess. Acting in hurts us and stifles us. We are no more supposed to target ourselves than to target others.

Question: If we are not to act outward, and we are not to act inward, and we aren't to retaliate, what are we to do?

Answer: Explore the impulse to retaliate.

The way through is to learn how to make room for and

positively contain, not suppress but contain, the impulse to retaliate.

We can't make room for something we're denying. If we don't let ourselves know about an impulse, we can't explore it. If we can't explore it, we can't learn from it.

Irritation is the halo of frustration. And irritation is separate from frustration. If you step on my toe, I feel irritated. It is the flare of energy that wants to protect me from being hurt any further.

My behavior, as a result of my irritation, could be an expression of hostility. "You stepped on my toe, you jerk. "

Each of these is separate. My hurt toe, my frustration, my irritation, and my expression—all separate. When I slow the whole process down, I can differentiate all the parts. And I can find the truth of what I really want to do. Get even. I want to step on the other guy's toe. I want him to feel the hurt he caused me.

This is what retaliation is about. I want you to feel the same feeling that I felt because of what you did.

The impulse to retaliate is very quick. It is quickly denied, especially in a Christian community. It is buried so deep that discovering it takes time.

We have ways of unearthing it. Each of the following is an opportunity to discover an edge of the retaliatory impulse.

- Exploring depression. Very likely, the pivotal moment between having energy and the onset of depression occurred when a retaliatory thought or impulse was suppressed.
- Exploring outrage. Sarcasm or righteous indignation are retaliation made legitimate by a rational ideal.
- Noticing intention movements.
- Noticing the suppression of intention movements.

- Noticing the impulse to retaliate

Once we notice some aspect of an impulse to retaliate, then we can explore it. And gaining awareness of our retaliatory impulses and learning how to explore rather than act on them gives us an entirely new relationship to the world. We gain parts of ourselves we had hitherto split off from our awareness, and each of those parts were hanging onto the energy required to keep them buried.

Here is the treasure. Ultimately, through this exploration, we discover, on a very deep level, aspects of ourselves we had lost without even realizing it.

We discover what was, on a deep level, done to us. We surface this wound and give it care. We heal. This makes all the difference in the world. It changes our world. It makes it whole.

Intention Movements[38]

An intention movement is a motion, usually subtle, that reveals the metaphor of retaliation. Group members are usually unaware of their slight intention movements, so the leader has to be paying close attention. A fist, a little kick, a hand moving backwards, a clenched jaw—these may be telegraphing the desire to punch, kick, slap, or bite.

The eye-opening phrase I've heard often in SCT groups is, "Your body knows something that your mind doesn't know yet."[39]

Christians hang out in their minds. They are thinkers. So they may rely more on thought than on physical clues. They may be unaware that their bodies are offering information.

The previous chapters of stair-step training, of learning to

---

[38] (Agazarian, SCT for Groups 1997), pp. 87-88.

[39] (Agazarian, SCT for Groups 1997), p. 211.

contain, are all important now. Now we want to make room for the body's wisdom. We want to invite the body to reveal to us its awareness of how we want to retaliate.

Making room here means pausing to allow the intention movement, to give it full scope. To allow the fist to punch the air, or the foot to kick out, or the hand to slash backward, or the jaw to grind.

An Example of Exploring the Retaliatory Impulse[40]

This process both surfaces the impulse and the metaphor contained within the impulse. As the member makes room for this physical expression of retaliation, no one is hurt; because it's the muscular movement and awareness of the energy driving it—not connecting with any target—that reveals the deep experience.

Exploring the Retaliatory Impulse	
Leader	**Member**
Are you aware that you are frowning?	No
Your body knows something your mind doesn't know yet. Are you curious about what your body knows?	Yes.
What does your body want to do?	Make a face.

---

[40] For a thorough discussion of varieties of retaliatory expression, revenge fantasies, and the process of change, see Chapter 9 of Systems-Centered Therapy for Groups, Agazarian, pp. 204-220.

Can you let your body make the face it wants to make?	[Member makes a wide grimace.]
What energy is being channeled into your face?	It's like hot wires traveling up my jaw and sparking out of my mouth.
What's it like, feeling that energy?	It actually feels good.
Make as much room as you can for your energy.	I actually do feel a lot of energy.
You seem to be discovering that you're okay while you feel this.	[Surprise.] I am OK!
[The leader and members pay close attention to the emergence of the metaphor.]	The sparks, like burning pinpricks.
Like flinging burning pinpricks. So this is how you felt.	Yes! Just like burning pinpricks were flung at me.

There. There's the nugget. The body was holding a metaphor, an extremely accurate metaphor, about what the personal harm was, and the only way to access the full accuracy, the full understanding of injury was to allow the retaliatory impulse to play out.

But how different it is to let it play out as a metaphor, an enacted metaphor, instead of acting it out, either verbally, or physically. The person does not have to actually deliver the grimace to whomever caused the original injury. It's making room for the motion that brings awareness of the energy.

Let's say the intention movement is a clenched jaw, representing a stifled desire to chew on somebody or a clenched fist, representing a stifled desire to punch somebody. If another person were actually chewed on or punched, it wouldn't work. In that case, and in all misdirected anger, the attention is on the target.

For transformation to occur, the attention has to be within oneself. One has to be looking inside and describing what is in there. Giving the physical enactment space opens that internal room.

Transformation is swift. Once the metaphor is released, once the energy is expressed, once the treasure is revealed, it's done. There might be a flurry of action, of fire, of fiery expression, and then? The anger is gone. A new place has been reached. It's a miraculous deliverance.

Bearing Witness

By exploring the impulse to retaliate, an injury is deeply noticed. The individual is, often for the first time, able to bear witness to the specific nature of an injury. The leader and the group are also witnesses. What was hidden is brought into the light.

This almost always is expressed as a metaphor, and it is almost always very specific and accurate with regard to the impact on the individual.

When a Christian community has these skills, they can better discriminate between true issues and issues that have to do with the authority phase of group development. Each person is holding his or her own unwitnessed issues, which influences his or her interpretation of events. And each person, and the congregation as a whole, is somewhere on the continuum of the phases of development.

Such complex interactions can either cause a mess or a transformational sorting out—if the community knows how to use these skills.

Congregational training meetings for practicing these tools give members an automatic method whenever another issue comes up. The more they practice, the more resilient they will become and the more capable of handling complexities.

What Ifs:

1. What if a member or a leader figures out the injury first, before the individual doing the work?

2. What if there's no obvious intention movement?

3. What if the retaliatory impulse is toward someone in the group?

4. What if the group gets frightened by the expression of aggression?

5. What if someone in the group isn't that glued together or can't make the distinction between metaphoric representative action versus actual violence?

1. **What if** the leader or a member catches on to another member's injury, before the member does?

Make room and be patient. Discovery has the most impact when the individual himself comes up with his own specific metaphor, *unless* the subgroup is working a common retaliatory impulse, in which case, each member will have his/her own metaphor and the join is sharing metaphors. The content of a metaphor does not have to be echoed, it's the process of pulling up the metaphor that is the join.

2. **What if** there's no obvious intention movement?

The leader can ask if any impulses are being tightened against.

Are you trying to *keep yourself* from doing anything? Are you keeping yourself from kicking? Do you notice making your hands stay still?

Someone complaining of having a tight throat, for example, may be keeping herself from saying impassioned words. Words are stuck in her throat. Exploring the tightness and what is being tightened against is a way in.

3. **What if** the aggression or retaliatory impulse is toward someone in the group?

The leader steps in as the target. The group won't be ready to handle direct expression of retaliatory metaphors until they have experience taking themselves all the way through the authority phase to the intimacy phase, and until they are fully capable of containing. Until then, the leader vectors the anger to herself/himself.

Leader Containing Aggression for Group	
Leader	**Member**
	I'm aware of wanting to retaliate against Tom.
What did I do?	Tom said...
What did I say?	Before we started, you said I had to move my car.
What did you want to do to me when I said that?	I wanted to shove your car over the cliff.
You wanted to teach me a lesson?	Yes, I wanted to teach you that you can't order everyone around.
Can you feel your arousal?	Yes
How does that feel?	I have a lot of energy. I like it.
Can you let yourself enjoy your energy?	Yes. I'm enjoying it.
Make lots of room for your energy.	Making room. It's taking up my whole body. I feel like I could move mountains, anybody else?

4. **What if** the group gets frightened by the expression of aggression?

Some members of the group are likely to be frightened by the emergence of aggression, especially when some of the metaphors describe violence.

Fear that is caused by a thought can be reduced by using the technique for testing the reality of a negative prediction.

As aggression starts to show up, watch for a subgroup that welcomes more honest expression and another subgroup that wants to run from aggression. Clearly, the group is then showing itself to be close to the transition between flight and fight as embodied in the two subgroups. The subgroups can work both sides of the issue each time aggression becomes more of a presence.

Despite the tremendous violence done to Jesus, and the presence of that violence in our religious art and symbols—in the crucifix, for example—violent metaphors are likely to strike a reaction.

At some point, someone will have a reaction to a violent metaphor, and that becomes, then, work for another subgroup. This leads to the important discrimination between metaphorical violence and actual violence, especially as members see and experience the transformation that metaphors create.

A person who is fearful of a violent metaphor may be a very visual person, able to visualize the violence all too clearly, may have been victimized by violence, or may be afraid of their own suppressed violence. Whatever aspect is presented, someone else in the group is bound to be able to join. As those members explore their take on the issue, other members will be working along and the group will become safer for this more intense type of discovery.

5. **What if** someone in the group isn't that glued together or can't make the distinction between metaphoric representative actions versus actual violence?

I admit all the Christian communities I've belonged to contained high functioning people. Their modus operandi ran far more to stifling themselves than acting out.

With a group on the other end of the spectrum, I'd suggest some sessions for subgrouping about the distinction between metaphoric and actual violence, perhaps trying out mild metaphoric actions first and noticing how it feels both to watch and to participate in such actions.

We certainly want our communities to be as inclusive as possible, but if someone in the group simply isn't emotionally equipped for this degree of interaction, then an alternative group, taking more time to learn these skills and applying them to lighter issues, could be a possibility.

Similarly, children and young people can learn to subgroup, and lighter versions of these principles and skills can be taught.

22 NOISE

As if it weren't enough to develop a comprehensive theory of living human systems, Dr. Agazarian also, with Anita Simon, came up with a System for Analyzing Verbal Interaction® (SAVI®).[41]

Yet another elegant offering, SAVI is a system for encoding and analyzing communication to identify patterns that promote or work against successful transfer of information.

We won't get into that here, beyond pointing out that the manner one communicates has an effect on others and the effectiveness of the communication. We have choices about how we put forward an idea or a statement. We can do it in a way that raises another person's hackles, triggering their fight energy, or we can do it in a way that enlists cooperation.

We can also lose listeners when our communication is noisy.

Shannon and Weaver defined noise as ambiguity, redundancy, or contradiction.[42] You can research it yourself by noticing what starts to happen inside you when someone talking to you is vague, repeats the same message with slight variation two or three times, or contradicts himself.

If group members introduce noise into the group, it can be an

---

[41] SAVI® is a registered trademark of Yvonne Agazarian, Claudia Byram, Fran Carter, and Anita Simon.

[42] Claude Shannon and Warren Weaver, *The Mathematical Theory of Communication*, Urbana, University of Illinois Press, 1971.

interesting and enlightening topic for subgrouping.

Do you notice that the subgroup is repeating itself? Who is noticing a reaction to that? Do we have two subgroups—One to explore the pull to repetition, the other to explore the effect of it?

23 MORE STAIR 5—ADAPTIVE ROLES

In any   situation, there are
                                            functional roles and adaptive roles.
            Thus far we've discussed roles that are functional—
member role, leader role—roles that involve operating in a way that
promotes the goals of both the group and the system within which
the group is nested.

The nesting looks like this:

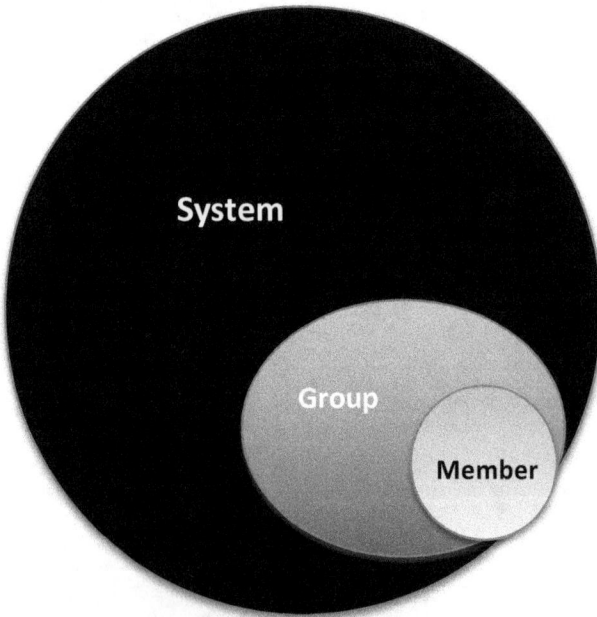

Members are nested in the group. The group is nested in the system.

Here's how it looks within the church:

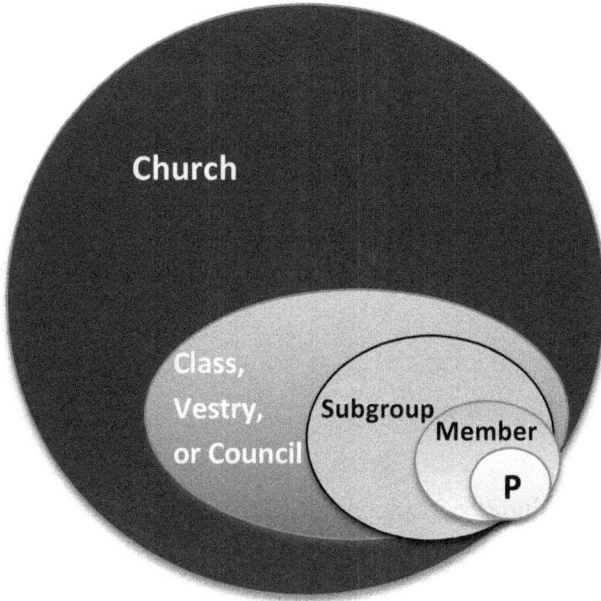

Members are nested in the subgroup, which is nested in the class (vestry, council, etc.). The class is nested in the church. To the extent the person has brought herself/himself across the boundary into a functional member role, the person is nested in the member.

Of course, the church is itself nested in the diocese, district, or synod, these divisions nested in the entire church organization, and the organization nested in Christianity (and Christianity nested in Christ Jesus).

We also, each of us, carry any number of adaptive roles, roles we adopted to adapt ourselves to (usually) our original system—the family. These roles can snap into place whenever we need a strategy to help ourselves when we are threatened.

Any number of things can be threatening, including life itself. Therefore, some of us may operate entirely out of an adaptive role without even realizing it.

When I was in college, my church group went to South Chicago to volunteer in a youth center for a time. I went into the kitchen and cooked. A cook was needed so my role was helpful but I was also buttressing myself against a situation beyond my skills—hanging out with my fellow group members in an unstructured situation full time. I had no trouble going to the youth center to lead children in an activity, but being with my peer crowd all day long required more social skill than I possessed.

For years, whenever a situation became too much, I'd head for the kitchen. Subsequently, I was exposed to ever more elegant training and no longer needed to hide myself in a task.

Recently, at a family passage, I was again in the kitchen, not hiding, but working rather seamlessly, and even joyfully, with my sister-in-law to handle a large family's large appetite. This time the role was a choice and a functional one.

Going to the kitchen was a "doing something" role that defended me against interpersonal interaction I wasn't ready for. Roles can take a variety of shapes and manifestations—actions, non-actions, attitudes, ways of thinking, sets of beliefs—so an occasion to discover and explore adaptive roles we might take in the church community is a powerful opportunity offered in few other places beyond a select few therapy offices.

Here I'm offering a bridge between unconsciously enacted adaptive roles in daily life and carefully unpacked role discovery in a savvy therapist's office.

From here on, in this chapter, when I refer to role, I'm referring to adaptive roles.

Adaptive roles are like entire worlds that enclose us, filtering our perception and splintering our skills. An image of this for me is a translucent ornament hung on a Christmas tree, and inside the ornament is a tiny me, looking through the glass darkly, perceiving only a portion of the reality, reacting to that distorted viewpoint, my usual skills locked outside the circumference.

Roles are triggered by something, usually something perceived as a threat. Most of us have an assortment of roles that can be triggered—victim, poor me, top dog, clown, jock, professor. We can be tripped into a role so quickly we don't even know we're there. But suddenly we're perceiving only the information that goes with that role and we've forgotten many of our advanced skills. A victim will mainly see threat. A professor will mainly see the script for the lecture. Poor me will see herself buried under a heap. Clown will see it all as humorous.

We are suddenly acting only from the role, and, very likely, triggering a reciprocal role in another person. In marriages this can lead to a role lock,[43] each person picking up a familiar role that dances with the other one. The couple is no longer operating member to member but role to role. And because it feels real and is extremely familiar, neither recognizes that their whole self is no longer available.

I remember running into an ex some years after our divorce. I could see many good qualities and wondered why I'd found him so lacking. I realized we no longer were relating to each other through our roles. Without the scrim of the role, I could see the actual decent person.

This stage is one where people may bow out. The longer we know someone and the more we are together, the more vulnerable we are to being triggered into a role. Without an understanding of adaptive roles, of the encompassing nature of a role, people can leave relationships, not realizing their view of the other person is

---

[43] (Agazarian, SCT for Groups 1997), p. 223.

being filtered through their own personal issues.

Roles are typically either one-up or one-down. We can find ourselves either in an underdog or a superior position, the follower or the resister, the trampler or the trampled upon, the server or the one being served, the helper or helpee.

When we learn to recognize and get ourselves out of an adaptive role, we can see how to interact more spontaneously with another person, even when that person is still in a role. It's an amazing freedom and, of course, a way we gain authority over our own participation in relationships.

The first challenge is detecting that you are even in a role. The passage into a role is so slick—role suction[44]—that we don't have any sensation of having been transported. And because we are now perceiving the world through the eyes of the role, it is hard to realize that our perception is now filtered.

We may feel that the situation is now desperate. We may feel powerful anger or sadness, or helplessness, or paralysis. We may feel as if there is no way out, that we've been here before and that we'll be stuck here forever. These feelings are probably quite intense.

Not only have we lost access to our full complement of skills, we don't even remember that we have wider skills.

Clues

Clues that can tell us that we're caught in an adaptive role:
- Intensity. The situation feels very intense.
- No way out. We can't see a way out. (In a one-up role, the way out is *our* way.)

---

[44] (Agazarian, SCT for Groups 1997), p. 224.

- Familiarity. We've been here before.
- Limited skills. We feel under-equipped for the situation. (In a one-up role, we believe we have superior skills.)
- Positional. We might be able to remember that we got to the other side of outrage or depression—acting outward or acting inward—and had anger. We might be able to remember that we entered the fight subphase.
- Threatened authority. We might feel that our personal authority as human beings is being threatened.

In our church group, the leader is now much needed. She/he, tracking our group's subphases of development, will remember that this is the defense that shows up after the group makes it through the transition from flight to fight. This is when group members will be triggered into one-up and one-down roles and have the opportunity to explore those roles and learn a great deal about themselves.

Role exploration builds on all the skills that have gone before. Some interesting characteristics of roles:

- They appear when they provide some function for the group.[45]
- Through their roles, members cue others to treat them in ways familiar to their personal adaptation.[46]
- Roles provide a stabilizing function, a way of containing conflict until it can be explored.[47]
- When the focus is the function of the role for the group, rather than the person playing the role, the group can

---

[45] Ibid, p. 221.

[46] Ibid, p. 221.

[47] Ibid, p. 222.

discover what is happening in the group that creates the need for the role.[48]

Exploring Roles [49]

While a church group was learning functional subgrouping, one new member took a stance of defiance around using this new tool in the group. Based on past behavior, the leader knew this member was susceptible to a defiant role.

Since you've honorably read the previous chapters, you know that the teaching of subgrouping occurs at the very beginning of group training. Therefore, you can deduce that in this case, the defiance showed up during the flight subphase.

Quiz: How did the leader respond?

Answer: True role exploration would be out of order, since this takes place in a much later subphase of group development. Therefore the leader said, "Anybody else? Do we have a subgroup of people who do not want to learn functional subgrouping?"

This response provided a container for all the people resistant to something or anything (or in hostage to flight) while the group was young, and it slipped them into helpful and reassuring behavior without their even noticing it. Thus they got to experience taking a defiant stand without standing alone, which gave the entire group an injection of energy.

This quiz points up the importance of remembering context. A leader's job is to recognize when an issue is arising that the group is not ready for, to recognize how the issue fits into the context of the

---

[48] Ibid, p. 223.

[49] SCT offers a detailed protocol for Undoing a Role within learning groups at conferences and role workshops.

group's readiness.

Of course people might operate from their roles any old time, not just when the group is ready for that type of work. So at any stage of the group's development, the leader will guide the group to subgroup an issue, after figuring out a way of presenting that issue in a lower octane if it is beyond the group's skill level.

We want our groups to be successful, which means we guide them in handling only those challenges they are prepared for.

A similar issue, arising when the group is ready for role work, would be responded to differently. If the group has reached this subphase, it already has had experience differentiating feelings from facts, reality testing, bracketing shifts in energy, and discovering and exploring its impulses.

Such skills are critical when looking into the encapsulated experience of a role, and the leader can be attentive to ways the group's process can provide a review of those skills as role-work approaches.

In any group, a time will likely come when some members are compliant and others defiant, two common roles. A compliant (or defiant) voice, appearing at this stair-step, is an opportunity and signal for the group to begin role work. Without doubt, someone else will offer the opposite voice. Each subgroup can then explore their side of compliance and defiance.

The leader can guide an individual or subgroup in making the following discriminations:[50]

- Awareness of being caught in a role.
    - o Role suction—a whoosh of being transported at

---

[50] Derived from the process outlined and demonstrated on pp. 232-233, *Systems-Centered Therapy for Groups*.

light speed into this small intense chamber of limited resources.

- *Are you feeling less than (or more than).*
- *Are you feeling constricted?*
- *Are you feeling rigid?*
- *Are your skills limited right now?*

- Thoughts
  - o Separating thoughts from experience.
    - *What did you think when you experienced that?*
- Feelings
  - o Separating feelings from thoughts.
    - *What did you feel when you thought that?*
- Trigger.
  - o Identifying the trigger
    - *What did you see or hear that catapulted you into the role?*
  - o Separating observations from interpretations.
    - *When you saw that, what did it mean to you?*
  - o Separating feelings from interpretations.
    - *What did you feel (your internal experience), as a result of your interpretation?*
- Reciprocal Pairing
  - o *What is the flip side of the role?*
    - Examples: compliance/defiance, martyr/persecutor, victim/rescuer, scapegoat/scapegoater.
  - o *When you are sucked into your role, what role might be triggered in another person?*
- Fork-in-the-Road
  - o *Which side of the pairing would you like to explore?*

Meanwhile, the leader must keep an eye out for whatever

current is circulating through the group that is triggering the emergence of a particular role or role-lock. For example, let's say martyr energy is appearing in the group. What is happening, that some members feel persecuted?

If you'll think for a moment about yourself, you know that there are times when your compliant energy is aroused and other times your defiant energy is aroused. Your body is a thermometer telling you the temperature of currents around you.

A temptation for group members will be to label or accuse someone of being defiant or compliant, or some other type of role label, such as victim or martyr. Remember to take it out of the personal and to remind them that the person holding a role is doing it for the group and that something must be going on that triggers the role. The group's job is to explore until they can discover what it is.

Toward the end of the exploration, most people will be out of their role and they can look objectively at what sent them into it.

Successful exit from a role gives important mastery over one's own processes. The more a role is examined, the less power it will have over time. With practice, roles lose their potency and members get better at catching themselves in the act of being triggered, capable of bypassing a role entirely and, instead, exploring the arousal caused by the trigger.

Eventually, individuals will discover that a role is a way they split off a part of themselves, either by transferring a rejected aspect into another person, or by splitting off the opposing aspect in order to stay safe.

For example, a person fearful of being scapegoated may tend to scapegoat others. They have split off the part of themselves that has experienced being a scapegoat and located that in another vessel—the other person.

Conversely, a person rejecting their own tendency or desire to scapegoat others may solve the problem by volunteering to be a scapegoat, locating the persecutor in another vessel—the other person.

Although I'm using rather common terminology here, the actual experience may call for a much more immediate name or label, determined uniquely by each person exploring within the subgroup. Leaders should be sensitive to unique names and use those, rather than a more clinical label.

For example, within a subgroup, members may use Trampled, Squished, Sat On, Freeze-dried as their personal names for being scapegoated. The leader should copy this lexicon, rather than force a generic label.

In a church community, having this common understanding and a way to support each other in getting out of a role gives unprecedented power, not just to the community but to the way individuals interact in their personal lives. Their stature grows.

24 ROLE WORK IN A BELL CHOIR

At a rehearsal, ringers actually began raising their voices toward a member. Afterwards, they had a training session.

Leader: "Who's aware of heightened energy in the group today?"

General assent.

Viva: "Hayd isn't damping. It drives me crazy."

Leader: "So you believe you are a superior ringer."

Viva: (hesitating) "Okay, yes, I secretly do."

Leader: "Do we have a superior ringer subgroup?"

Moze: "I see myself as an excellent ringer. I sight-read well. I ring exactly on time. I rarely miss a key change. Anybody else?"

Viva: "I join you on enjoying my musicality. I love how good I am. And I love it when our ensemble is performing well. I forget the mechanics and just enjoy the music. Anybody else?"

Salie: "I join on enjoying the music and forgetting the mechanics. I notice that after awhile, I don't even really see the music. It's like it's played through me. Anybody else?"

Viva: "So that's why it's so jarring when Hayd doesn't damp. I want him to pay attention..."

Leader: "So can you tell if a role is pulling you in, Viva?"

Viva: "This is reality. We have to damp between notes or the tones get muddy. This is bell-ringing 101."

Leader: "So you feel more than, better than?"

Viva: "Yes."

Leader: "What did you experience, when Hayd didn't damp?"

Viva: "Irritation."

Leader: "What did you think about being irritated?"

Viva: "I thought I shouldn't be irritated. We're sitting in a church right now."

Leader: "What did you feel when you thought you shouldn't be irritated in a church?"

Viva: "Wrong. Bad. And then I felt stifled and angry."

Leader: "So then what did you think?"

Viva: "I thought if Hayd would only damp, I wouldn't be going through this."

Leader: "So you blamed Hayd for your discomfort? What was the trigger? What did you see or hear that catapulted you into the role?"

Viva: "Director Stave reminded us to damp and even held the end of the note on measure 24 for, like, 15 minutes, and Director Stave never said, 'Hayd, your bell is still sounding.'"

Leader: "Did you have a thought at that point?"

Viva: "I thought Director Stave was being too nice. He kept being generic, issuing a general statement, instead of being direct and speaking to Hayd."

Leader: "How did you interpret this?"

Viva: "I thought he was protecting Hayd."

Leader: "What did this mean to you?"

Viva: "That he's placing Hayd's needs above the needs of the rest of us to perform well."

Leader: "Can you see that your interpretation is separate from your observation of Director Stave's behavior?"

Viva: "Yes."

Leader: "So this sequence was the trigger for what?"

Viva: "I can see I got into a 'more deserving' role. I deserve more consideration because I'm a superior ringer."

Leader: "Well done. Are you in that role now?"

Viva: "No."

Leader: "What role do you think gets triggered in someone else, if you are in a more deserving role?"

Viva: "Less deserving."

Leader: "Do you have a less deserving side too, that you sometimes go to?"

Viva: "Yes, but I don't like going there. I'd rather hang out with the more deserving side of myself."

Leader: "Which one do you want to explore right now?"

Viva: "The more deserving side. Anybody else?"

And with that, the *more deserving* subgroup was launched. Later, the less deserving subgroup worked and, part way through, Viva was able to join that subgroup and do some important work.

The leader had certain decision points. (Actually a leader is constantly making decisions about which direction to go and what skills to pull in.)

The leader saw that one-up energy was in the group and first encouraged a subgroup to explore the experience of being a 'superior ringer.' The draw of the role was strong and pulled the member back into it.

The leader could have, if the group hadn't gotten good at self-observation, vectored the group toward undoing the mind reads about either Hayd or Director Stave. A group beyond stair-step 3 but not yet at stair-step 5 could have explored irritation and the impulse to either act out or act in.

This group's proficiency and experience made it possible to tackle the role head-on, achieving insights that could only be found by taking the role apart bit by bit.

As you can see, boundaries are inserted that bring clarity. A boundary was placed between observations and thoughts, another boundary between thoughts and interpretations, and another between interpretations and feelings. With each new boundary and separation, something else was discovered, until an encompassing insight moved Viva beyond the role into brand-new territory of self-seeing.

It's when thoughts, feelings, reactions, interpretations, and internally held rules get all mushed together, that a conglomerate mess ensues—a role—one that, beneath Viva's radar, was driving her.

Viva, when she started the exploration, had no idea that an avoidance of her own undeserving side was behind her one-up position. She did not know she was in a role. ("This is reality. We have to damp between notes or the tones get muddy. This is bell-ringing 101.") Her statement shows she felt totally justified in her stance.

What a difference, then, when she worked her way to re-claiming her own split-off side.

By exploring a role, you become more yourself, pasting yourself back together, creating a reunion of a piece of you that has been tucked away for, perhaps, decades.

I hope you can see how this supports you in refreshing your authority over your own possibilities.

FAQ

Question. How is it that the Leader worked with Viva instead of through the subgroup?

Answer. This is often how a new skill is introduced to a group. When the group demonstrates that it is on a leading edge—as here by surfacing one-up energy—the leader takes the opportunity to teach a new skill. This is done with a member who has shown proficiency in the preceding skills. This particular member then becomes a model for the group, trying something out on the group's behalf.

The group always watches this closely, taking it in, applying it to themselves, working along, and soon this skill is owned by the group, becoming a part of the group's culture and each individual's skillset.

25 STAIR 6 AND COUNTING

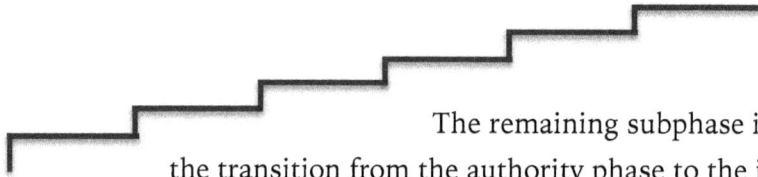

The remaining subphase involves the transition from the authority phase to the intimacy phase. This subphase includes the crisis of hatred and resistance to change either through targeting authority or targeting self. Stubbornness and suspicion rear their heads, directed either toward an authority, who is seen as the cause of all the problems, or toward oneself, seeing oneself as incompetent or weak.[51]

The dilemma for both the group and the leader is that the group leader/trainer will come under fire and the group will be resistant to help from the leader. The effectiveness of passage through the prior stair-steps is what will make the difference. If the group has learned to contain aggression in subgroups, it will be able to contain the fire of this passage. If the group has two leaders, one can help while the other is targeted. (But neither leader will be exempt.)

It is critically important for the leader to not break any boundaries during this time.[52] Even during this subphase, the leader is a container for the group. If, say, the leader is even slightly

---

[51] (Agazarian and Gantt, Autobiography 2000), p. 208.

[52] (Agazarian, SCT for Groups 1997), p. 108.

late, the group's faith in its container is shaken.

Some members might want to caretake the leader by offering solace outside the group meeting; for example, an invite to coffee or a listening ear.

Leaders, don't succumb. Find your support from a mentor or peer, not someone in the group. Your group has almost reached intimacy. Don't blow it.

It will be tempting. After the group has enacted firing squad behavior, a warm human touch looks pretty good. Go get it, just not from a member.

FAQ

Q. So after you reach the Intimacy Phase, does it get easy? Are we done?

A. The Intimacy Phase also has subphases in which members work through defenses against individuation and separation. [53] These are challenging enough to send some group members back to the authority phase as more palatable ground.

Q. I suppose this means the Interdependent Love and Work Phase also has tasks?

A. Yes, people get to encounter their defenses against knowledge and common sense.[54]

Q. Does it ever end?

A. That's a question, isn't it? The possibility of further development never does seem to end on this side of the veil, thank goodness. I've found the joy of discovering and healing ever more

---

[53] (Agazarian and Gantt, Autobiography 2000), p. 209.

[54] Ibid.

of myself as living with SCT principles continues. I'm offered more choices, more perspective, and more outright fun as I make ever clearer decisions thanks to my training. Whether we continue to have issues on the other side—well, I plan to enter that phase with curiosity, and wonder.

26 CLIMBING THE STAIRCASE

Each time the group comes together, it starts with the first stairs and moves through the tasks that allow it to climb higher. As it gets stronger with each set of skills, its ability to move gracefully upward will expand. The leader continues to contain any difficult energy until the members can do it themselves.

Obviously, the first passes will occur at a lighter level and on later passes, the group will gain the capacity to explore at ever deeper levels. A leader's job becomes more and more delightful as the group begins to enjoy the process, trust the efficacy of the techniques, and learns to contain its energy.

As members gain mastery over their own ability to take and give authority appropriately, it leads to increased facility in fulfilling the church's mission. The community's ability to discriminate will be impressive and they'll have energy for the goals of the church.

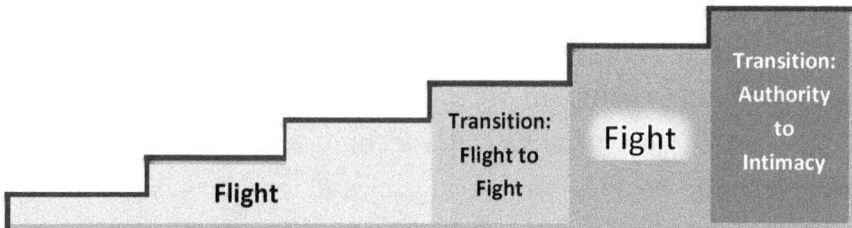

Flight

Transition: Flight to Fight

Fight

Transition: Authority to Intimacy

27 THE LEADER ROLE

The leader is a juggler, keeping several balls in the air at once.

- Holding the boundaries—respecting time and space, here and now, and process boundaries.
- Training the group when they are ready for each new level of skill and defense modification.
- Intervening when subgrouping gets sloppy.
- Tracking who is in what subgroup.
- Noting which are the silent members.
- Paying attention to the group's position in the phases of group development and altering interventions accordingly.
- Detecting when the group is doing well, even if not perfectly, and staying out of the way.
- Noticing if they've actually found their solution, and missed it.

Most of the time, when a group reaches a revelation, there's a stunned, appreciative silence, but sometimes the energy is so high, they roll over it. That's a fun intervention for the leader: "Did you notice you found a solution?"

The leader role when using SCT techniques is a strong and active one. She/he does not just sit back and let things happen and see where they will go. An unguided group will sink into stereotypical behavior, dump unpleasant energy on scapegoats, caretake the person who volunteers to be the identified patient, and fall into compliance with the loudest person, or the person with the most investment in being seen as the leader.

In the old style of psychotherapy groups, such chaos was seen as useful, but the troubled church community is not a therapy group, rather a group of well-meaning individuals with a difficult task and varying levels of interpersonal skills. (And leading edge therapy groups bypass the suffering engendered by the old methods.)

As the leader teaches the hierarchy of skills, the group becomes better at problem-solving, handling ever more complex issues, and integrating differences. It becomes startlingly resourceful.

However, the leader must be strong. Holding to the process, patiently injecting *anybody else*, containing energy the group is not ready for, deciding when to intervene and when to teach the next skill, takes powerful attunement.

Each time the group climbs the stair-steps, they'll get better at it, and capable of accessing and handling more potent issues. As they start to trust the process and see where it takes them, they'll want to go forward. They will build on their previous work and become ever safer.

Some of the hard places for the leader are:

- Stepping forward to contain the angry energy of the group by encouraging a member to direct anger toward yourself rather than toward another group member.
- Remembering to not take the group's anger personally. (They are working out their authority issues and you are the group's authority.)
- Becoming curious about your own reactions even as you are guiding members to express their angry metaphors.
- Watching out for also being triggered into a role or role-lock.
- Handling actual anger or hatred that is directed toward you.

The first time the group is angry with the leader, they are like cubs mock fighting. They are trying out anger at the leader and they are trying you out. They are testing whether or not it is actually safe to be angry with you. The next time they are angry, they will truly be angry. Continue to listen and to lift up the metaphors.

The goal is still to discover the metaphor that reveals their deep experience of injury and, of course, you didn't cause that. Hang in as best you can. Don't turn on the group, watch that you're not triggered, and don't retaliate with heavy authority. Some groups want to draw blood and if you can put that into words, it helps them see themselves. *"You want to draw blood."*

Having two leaders is especially advantageous now. The other one can step in and guide the process while you're under fire.

If you handle this even moderately well—very few leaders handle this perfectly—you will gain the group's respect. They will trust you and, in the future, work even more powerfully.

Remember the sacred bowl exercise?

Question: What was the sacred bowl?

Answer: It was a container.

Look back over all the skills and tools taught to the group. What does each tool do? It provides for either discrimination or containment, sometimes both.

Step back far enough and we can see the intensely spiritual nature of this work. The members are learning to be containers for themselves and others.

And the leader, the leader is the container for the group. The group is gradually expanding its ability to embrace its fuller expression of being human, and on its way there, the leader is doing the holding. The leader is containing whatever the group isn't ready for.

I see the parallel to what Jesus did for us. Jesus contained sin and error for us. He was and is the container while we are challenged to strengthen our own capacity to be containers for ourselves and each other.

And what was the struggle that Jesus faced? The question of authority. Rome and the religious hierarchy were each asserting their authority over the threat presented by Jesus's presence and teaching. Even before Jesus was born, Herod tried to protect his authority from the potential Jesus would bring into the world.

And the Garden of Eden? Again, wrestling for authority.

We've been trying to work out authority since the world was born, so getting conscious about the process and practicing skills that advance containment is a completely worthy, and spiritual, endeavor.

Jesus is probably the only one who did this perfectly. He never seemed to lose perspective, even at his hardest times. He saw the flaws of his group members and stayed compassionate.

We can't expect such stellar behavior for ourselves, even if we've been trained extensively, but training does help, and to weather the subphases that target the leader, I encourage you to take in the opportunities offered by SCT events and literature.

28 THE CHURCH AS A WHOLE

Your Christian community, by practicing these skills on an ongoing basis, will become more and more whole and increasingly capable of embracing its shadow side, containing anger in a positive way. Targeting will decrease, and humor and lightness increase, as members get good at using their tools to take themselves to the heart of each thing that matters.

Obviously, a group can climb these steps over and over with each coming together for any purpose.

Energy will become increasingly available for the actual work of the church. And each family will be benefitted by the increased skillfulness of family members. Your Christian community will become a powerful witness to the efficacy of a spiritual life.

Resources

Agazarian, Y.M. (2010). *Systems-centered theory and practice: The contribution of Yvonne Agazarian* (Edited by SCTRI). Livermore, CA: WingSpan Press. Reprint (2011). London, UK: Karnac Books.

Gantt, S.P. , & Agazarian, Y.M. (Eds.) (2006). *Systems-centered therapy: In clinical practice with individuals, families and groups.* Livermore, CA: WingSpan Press. Reprint (2011). London, UK: Karnac Books.

Agazarian, Y.M. (2006). *Systems-centered practice: Selected papers on group psychotherapy.* London, UK: Karnac Books.

Gantt, S.P., & Agazarian, Y.M. (Eds.) (2005). *SCT in action: Applying the systems-centered approach in organizations.* Lincoln, NE: iUniverse. Reprint (2006). London, UK: Karnac Books.

Agazarian, Y.M. (1997). *Systems-centered therapy for groups.* New York, NY: Guilford. Reprint (2004). London, UK: Karnac Books.

Agazarian, Y.M. (2001). *A systems-centered approach to inpatient group psychotherapy.* London, UK & Philadelphia, PA: Jessica Kingsley.

Agazarian, Y.M., & Gantt, S.P. (2000). *Autobiography of a theory,* London, UK: Jessica Kingsley.

Agazarian, Y.M., & Peters, R. (1981). *The visible and invisible group.* London, UK: Routledge & Kegan Paul. Reprint (1987). London, UK: Karnac Books.

Shannon, Claude, and Weaver, Warren, *The Mathematical Theory of Communication,* Urbana, University of Illinois Press. 1971.

Website: www.systemscentered.com

About Anne Katherine

Anne Katherine has been guiding individuals and groups to fuller humanity for over forty years, first through her practice as a psychotherapist and then through her workshops, programs and books.

She holds an MA in psychology, various certifications, and completed University of the South's Education for Ministry in 1980.

Although she has retired from private practice, she is still writing full time, mostly screenplays.

She has eleven books, including this one, in print.

Her website is www.1annekatherine.com.